*The Hidden Story of
Scientology*

The Hidden Story of
SCIENTOLOGY

Omar V. Garrison

The Citadel Press   *Secaucus, N. J.*

Third printing, January 1975
Copyright © 1974 by Omar V. Garrison
All rights reserved
Published by Citadel Press
A division of Lyle Stuart, Inc.
120 Enterprise Ave., Secaucus, N. J. 07094
Manufactured in the United States of America
Library of Congress catalog card number: 74-80818
ISBN 0-8065-0440-4

"Any new vital force in the world has a hard time."

L. RON HUBBARD

Acknowledgements

The ultimate value of any work of investigative reporting depends to a large degree on the co-operation of honest and forthright informants, who supply the source material upon which it is based. This book is no exception.

Accordingly, the author wishes to express his gratitude to all who have provided data which clarify and support this work's central argument.

O. V. G.

Contents

Foreword

This book makes no pretence of being an authoritative work on the doctrine and practices of Scientology. How could it be, in all honesty, when I am not and never have been, a Scientologist?

I have never been processed nor dianetically audited, with or without the use of an E-meter. I cannot lay valid claim to the insights and independence of thought which are said to result (and I believe they do) from the proper application of Scientology's Standard Tech.

I must make this perfectly clear at the outset to forestall the inevitable allegation by people hostile to Scientology that Mr. Hubbard or his followers have "brainwashed" me or otherwise deprived me of my free will and common sense.

All this is not to say, of course, that I know little or nothing about the philosophy, aims and techniques of Scientology. I know a great deal about all of these, having made a careful and exhaustive study of the literature published by Scientology organizations themselves, as well as a great deal of material opposed to or attacking Scientology. In addition, I have enjoyed face-to-face discussions hours on end with well-informed Scientologists in America and abroad.

However, my underlying purpose in thus familiarizing myself with the history and practice of Scientology was orientation. It was preliminary to my real task, which has been to investigate charges made by Scientologists that there exists a world-wide, secret alliance, with interlocking national organizations, whose common goal is the establishment of a strictly controlled, one-world society.

The Scientologists further assert that they are being subjected to relentless attack by this "global conspiracy" because Scientology has challenged their aims and exposed their methods.

I paused a long time before that word *conspiracy*. Over and over again, we have had urged upon us the notion that people who believe they are the target of a conspiracy are victims of some kind of mental illness.

A mass-circulation magazine some time past published a long article on the subject, accompanied by a garish illustration depicting the many kinds of "conspiracies" some Americans, for example, believe to exist. The writer of the article hastened to note that it was only a minority of "the more alert among us" who view with suspicion much that is happening in our society today.

His meaning was clear: such persons are paranoiacs, suffering from what might be called a conspiracy syndrome.

He did not seem to think that the growing, bare-fisted threats to what most people consider civilized values might justify at least a modest amount of suspicion.

Still, there was a modicum of truth in his premise. In today's world of shifting verbal sands, when semantic slight-of-hand is widely used for everything from promoting cold-water detergents to the selling of a President, you can't be too careful about words. For, ultimately, words convey ideas; and ideas are as explosive as nitroglycerine.

According to the French thinker, Fouillée, every idea consists not only in an intellectual act, but also in what he terms "a certain direction of the sensibility and of the will". He believed that, as a consequence, "in society, as in the individual, every idea is a force, tending more and more to realise its individual end".

Writing of the vital role played by ideas in the French Revolution, Wyndham Lewis observed:

"It was seen how, properly used, they could burst open kingdoms and disintegrate societies, so that sons would massacre their fathers and virtuous women carouse with street-walkers and mix blood with their wine . . ."[1] (p. 65).

In our own day, a good illustration of this same phenomenon (if I may be allowed a brief digression) is the now-familiar idea of a "generation gap".

This expression, embodying the notion that an unbridgeable gulf of understanding and mores separates people on opposite sides of the arbitrary age of 29 years, 29 days, 59 minutes and 59 seconds, was fabricated by the hoax manufacturers of the revolutionary corporation in America.

Packaged, labelled and put on the intellectual market, it was vigorously promoted by the trained seals of journalism, the *en rapport* educators, the progressive clergy, the go-ahead psychologists and the *avant-garde* arbiters of cultural life.

The public, long accustomed to an uncritical acceptance of any authoritative broadside, soon made the idea a household commodity. Every dinner conversation, every Parent-Teacher Association meeting, every TV Talk Show was studded with references to the "generation gap". It was the latest thing. Similarly, the academic and literary air was suddenly full of the same phantasy.

Once the idea was in general circulation, it began to shape itself into reality. Parents discovered that, sure enough, they *couldn't* talk to their children any more and be understood or taken seriously. And youngsters above the age of twelve all parroted the same averment they had heard so often: there's no use trying to talk to your parents. They won't listen, and they don't know what it's all about, anyway.

Created and encouraged thus by the mythmakers, and

aided in its growth by the widest possible exposure in the mass media, the counter-culture of youth so confidently proclaimed, began indeed to emerge.

In cities and campuses across America, then across the world, appeared hordes of pathetic young tramps who had mistaken filth for freedom and drug-induced euphoria for "liberating experience".

Their mystique of deformity included various tribes and orders: the Yippies, the New Left radicals, the student-power organizers, the black militants dressed in the garb of African chiefs, and all the rest. Their slogans varied, but their goals were identical – destruction of civilized values. Their stampede was towards the abyss.

Allen Ginsberg, poet-spokesman for the new breed, wrote: 'I saw the best minds of my generation destroyed by madness, starving, hysterical, naked."

The power of words to unbalance and polarize society was never more clearly demonstrated. No wonder the process has been called by those who employ it "restructuring the social order through a revolutionary use of language".

But let us return to the word *conspiracy*. I owe it to my readers to clarify, so far as I am able, what is meant in this book by that term. Otherwise, what I have to say might get lost in disagreement as to what the term implies.

Scientologists well understand this point. Opposite the title page of most Scientology texts there appears an "An Important Note", which cautions the reader: "Always get any word or phrase you do not understand defined. Trying to read past a misunderstood word will result in mental 'fogginess' and difficulty in comprehending the following pages."

That is good advice for the reader of almost any non-fiction book today. For the purposes of the present inquiry, then, I have adopted the standard dictionary definition of *conspiracy*.

Webster's International gives, as one connotation, "a combination of men for an evil purpose; a plot".

The *Oxford Dictionary of English* agrees in this instance with the American usage, defining conspiracy as "a combination of persons for an evil or unlawful purpose; an agreement between two or more to do something criminal, illegal or reprehensible; a plot".

If, as the Scientologists claim, it can be shown that hidden enemies have knowingly combined their efforts in a plot to destroy Scientology, then on the basis of the definition just cited, a conspiracy does indeed exist.

From the outset, it appeared that the Scientologists have a prima facie case in the simple fact that they have been attacked without any just cause by the governments of every country in which they have had an organized following. These attacks have not taken the form of legal prosecution for violation of any existing laws. Rather, they have been launched as extra-legal acts of oppression, of the kind familiar to anyone who has followed the rigged hearings and judicial proceedings set in motion by Soviet authorities when dealing with "enemies of the State".

I have read through thousands of pages of transcript covering such hearings, official enquiries and parliamentary debates in the U.S., Australia, South Africa, Rhodesia, New Zealand, Canada and Britain. Yet in not a single instance that I have been able to discover have any of these lengthy proceedings produced a shred of evidence that Scientologists or Scientology's founder have been guilty of anything actionable under the criminal or civil laws of the countries conducting them.

Instead, the most serious indictment to emerge from the vast heaps of verbiage is a vague generalization such as "Scientology is an evil cloud", or "Scientology is a falsehood and a fantasy".

Even Britain, the most permissive country in Western Europe, banned foreign Scientologists from entering the

United Kingdom because they were – (are you ready for it?) – "socially harmful".

Here was the tight little island, in whose major cities crimes of all categories were steadily increasing exponentially each year, with no effective action taken to curb them.

More than a hundred Soviet Communist spies, whose presence and activities had been known to Whitehall for four years, were finally expelled only when a defector from the Russian KGB (secret police) let the cat out of the bag. If British traitors had been aiding them, they were never apprehended.

Pornographers were flourishing, sometimes with official assistance. For example, the Department of Trade and Industry – a governmental agency – agreed to pay a subsidy to the publisher of *The Little Red Schoolbook*, earlier found by the courts to be obscene, so he could exhibit the volume at the Frankfurt Book Fair.

Independent investigation had uncovered shocking evidence that patients in certain British mental institutions were being grossly abused. But a government white paper blithely dismissed the report as being based on "misrepresentations, wilful disregard of medical opinion, and serious distortion of facts".

Subsequent to this demurrer, not one but several mental hospitals were involved in serious scandals, as we shall detail in a later chapter.

Against this background of official tolerance almost to the point of idiocy, Scientology – a religious philosophy aimed at the spiritual regeneration of mankind – was viewed as "socially harmful".

In other countries, events followed a similar course. Although Scientology was only a minor sect, the massive powers of national governments were arrayed against it.

In the United States, the interventionist character of the government made it possible to attack Scientology in a brutal and direct way. The instrumentality for these assaults was the federal agencies such as the Food and Drug

Administration, the Internal Revenue Service, the Post Office Department, and the Federal Trade Commission.

Using the totalitarian (but unconstitutional) police powers they now wield in America, these bureaucratic hierarchies have tried to suppress Scientology by administrative law and by extra-legal harrassment.

Viewed objectively, the marshalling of such awesome forces against a small religious community appears decidedly fishy.

Another suspicious feature of the attacks on Scientology is that they all conform to a set pattern, regardless of the country in which they are carried out.

In each instance, the groundwork for official action is laid by a smear campaign in the media. Newspapers carry lengthy accounts purporting to show that a considerable number of people are being duped and their mental health undermined by a new "cult" called Scientology.

These initial stories carry headlines such as: "Scientology in South Africa Worries Doctors"; or, "Scientology Is Dangerous, Intellectuals Seriously Warn". Upon careful reading, the articles which follow turn out to be not news reports, but accounts of what are known to professional journalists as "pseudo-events", that is, interviews with biased "experts", aimed at swaying public opinion.

Next come sex and scandal stories (" 'Women Quizzed Me On Sex,' Says Schoolboy"); loaded opinion surveys; letters to the editor; cartoons derisive of Scientology; and exposés by spies who posed as students.

The succeeding stage involves carefully controlled and slanted debates on television and discussion forums, usually sponsored by organizations hostile to Scientology.

Once Scientology has been established in the public mind as something evil and a serious threat to the community, demands are made that the government "do something".

In Britain and Commonwealth countries, politicians "respond to growing concern", (i.e., they yield to pressure by certain individuals and groups), and put down a question

2—HSOS • •

in Parliament, then press for an enquiry into the practice and effects of the "dangerous cult".

Readers who are accustomed (or is it *conditioned?*) to a low-key, "balanced" discussion of all controversial issues, will no doubt regard this book as being strongly biased in favour of the Scientologists.

Let me say at once that the unequivocal conclusions stated herein were arrived at after more than a year of careful investigation and rest solely upon the documented evidence presented to support them.

I take no particular pleasure in being provocative; but I resolved that the disquieting import of this work would not be lost amid polite debate and tippy-toe assertions.

The possibility that any international alliance could extend its coercive power anywhere in the world; could use press, parliaments, ministries and diplomatic services to do its bidding, is too sobering a thought to dismiss lightly.

Who, then, are the individuals and groups that allegedly make up such a behind-the-scenes confederacy, if it does in fact exist? What are their over-all aims and why are they so violently opposed to Scientology?

In the following pages, I will attempt to supply at least partial answers to these questions and to others related to them. But to provide the reader with the perspective necessary to understand fully all that has happened and is still happening, it is necessary first to examine briefly the history and teachings of Scientology and of the science from which it evolved – Dianetics.

REFERENCE NOTES

1. Wyndham Lewis, *The Writer and the Absolute*. London: 1938.

1. *A Look at Dianetics*

To understand fully the meaning and methods of Scientology, it is necessary to know something of Dianetics, its forerunner and the technical foundation upon which it rests.

Dianetics came suddenly into public view in 1950. Yet it would be absurd to imagine that it was a spontaneous creation which before that date did not exist. As a matter of fact, years of experiment and research preceded the published work. Hubbard has said that he began his preliminary investigation to determine the dynamic principle of existence in 1932. His initial premise was that "the human mind is capable of resolving the problem of the human mind".

During the ensuing years, an intensive programme of study and testing (interrupted by World War II) evolved the fundamental techniques later embodied in Dianetics.

Hubbard published his *Original Thesis*, summarizing his findings, in 1948. Two years later, the basic text, *Dianetics: The Modern Science of Mental Health*, made its appearance in the literary market-place.

Although issued without fanfare and under the imprint of a minor New York publishing house, the book's success was instantaneous. Within weeks it had risen to the top of the best-seller list, that barometer of popular acclaim; and it became the most widely discussed book in America. Yet, before its unannounced advent in the book stores, the reading public had never even heard the word Dianetics which was, like the new mental science it denoted, the original creation of the book's author.

What is also interesting to note at this point is that while it had required a whole generation for the salient ideas and terminology of Freud's work on psychoanalysis to seep through to the man in the street, the fundamental thesis and vocabulary of Dianetics caught on in a matter of months.

Such massive and intense interest in the work by people in all walks of life suggests that it contained something the world had been waiting for and needed. What was it?

The word Dianetics was derived from the Greek *dia* meaning through, and *nous* meaning mind, hence "through the mind". The Dianetics system was described as the basic science of human thought.

"Dianetics is an adventure," wrote Hubbard in a brief foreword to his work. "It is an exploration into *Terra Incognita*, the human mind, that vast and hitherto unknown realm an inch back of our foreheads."

As it turned out, the itinerary and route map he provided for that strange journey were surprisingly accurate. Hubbard had closed his introduction with the words "may you never be the same again", and few who seriously undertook the adventure ever were. The only common ground shared by friend and foe of Dianetics has been, in fact, the agreement that "it works".

The principal reason for this is no doubt the fact that Hubbard had adopted an engineering approach to a subject which hitherto had been dealt with only by the deep, deep theories of established psychiatry, which led nowhere.

Early detractors had tried to counter the instant success of Dianetics by implying that the whole thing was a smoke-ring fantasy tossed off in his spare time by a science fiction writer named L. Ron Hubbard.

In fact, right down to the present, almost every published attack on Hubbard has included sneering references to his having written "wonder stories". His critics hoped thereby to plant in the public mind the idea that Dianetics is merely an extension of science fiction.

Even if this were true (and there is no evidence that it is) I cannot see that it would in any way degrade Dianetics as a scientific system. The voyage of Apollo II, the fantastic trail of human footsteps across the face of the moon, the terrifying mushroom cloud above the desert sands – all these achievements likewise made their first appearance in the pages of publications like *Astounding Science Fiction*. Only the writers of science fiction foresaw and described them in amazingly accurate detail.

That is why science fiction is the only fiction that is truly relevant to the present and the future.

In any case, Hubbard was not only an imaginative fictioneer, but among other things a civil engineer, explorer, former U.S. Navy officer, and licensed master of both motor and sailing vessels.

While all his published biographies take note of these and other attainments, none of them mentions the most important datum of all: L. Ron Hubbard is also a genius.

Until that fact is duly taken into account, much confusion and misunderstanding will continue to surround the man and his work.

From his earliest years, Hubbard's life and personal characteristics follow a pattern that has been typical of men who have made creative contributions to the sum of human knowledge, from the ancient Greek proto-scientists like Archimedes, down to the unknown Newtons and Faradays of our time, now tinkering with some new idea that will startle and perhaps outrage tomorrow's orthodox scientists.

Throughout history, the most conspicuous trait of genius has been a sense of wonder, or, in a more prosaic way of expressing it, a lively curiosity. Arthur Koestler, in his stimulating study, *The Act of Creation*, cites a passage from Aristotle in which the philosopher, speaking of the Greek men of science, says:

"At first they felt wonder about the more superficial problems; afterwards they advanced gradually by perplexing themselves over greater difficulties . . .'

As we shall see, that is precisely how Dianetics was evolved and how Hubbard advanced gradually from Dianetics into the greater problems and experiments of Scientology.

But it is not only in this single feature that Hubbard's personality matches the profile of genius. Other aspects of his behaviour and temperament similarly conform to the basic pattern: the enthusiasm over his work, the spontaneous flow of images and ideas; a mind pullulating with new notions; a scepticism towards dogmatic answers to pivotal questions.

Koestler further calls our attention to the fact that more often than not, men of genius have been self-assertive if not arrogant. Archimedes cried, "Give me but a firm spot on which to stand and I will move the earth." Tycho de Brahe, astronomer and pioneer of the scientific revolution, was "boastful, truculent and quixotic", and quarrelled even with kings he entertained at his table.

Pasteur infuriated his scientific adversaries by his self-confident attitude and the curt way in which he dismissed their scepticism concerning his theories: "You do not know the first word of my investigations, of their results, of the principles which they have established . . ."

Like these men, Hubbard is a fighting cock.

Still, beneath a veneer of overwhelming self-confidence will be found an ultimate humility, "derived from a sense of wonder close to mysticism . . ."; for mysticism figures in the motivational drive of almost all creative minds.

"In the popular imagination, these men of science appear as sober ice-cold logicians, electronic brains mounted on dry sticks. But if one were shown an anthology of typical extracts from their letters and autobiographies with no names mentioned, and then asked to guess their profession, the likeliest answer would be: a bunch of poets or musicians of a rather romantically naive kind."[1]

It is only the imitators, the third-rate minds, which seek security in authoritative doctrines and textbook infallability.

Like the wandering scholars of the Renaissance, who used to journey about Europe exploring many curious byways of knowledge before settling down to the study that would lead to new discoveries, Hubbard travelled widely during his youth, visiting some of the remoter areas of Asia. During the course of these peregrinations he says he observed many strange people and things which stimulated his interest in the unsolved riddles of existence: "the medicine man of the Goldi people of Manchuria, the shamans of North Borneo, Sioux medicine men, the cults of Los Angeles, and modern psychology. Amongst the people questioned about existence were a magician whose ancestors served in the court of Kublai Khan and a Hindu who could hypnotize cats."[7]

Hubbard adds that he also dabbled in the occult; examined the phenomena of spiritualism and studied the theories of celebrated psychologists like Freud, Adler and Jung.

Everybody and everything seemed to offer a partial solution to the basic problems confronting man, but none of them had evolved what Hubbard considered a workable system — one that yielded reliable results in the way demanded by an engineer who constructs a bridge. If an engineer were to employ as his parameters the kind of opinions, guesswork and uncertain methods common among psychologists and mystics, bridges would fall, buildings collapse, dynamos stall and civilization go to pieces.

Hubbard's first step in developing a workable system of his own was to look for a dynamic principle that would be the lowest common denominator of existence. He reasoned that all life is energy of some sort, and he asked the question: what is that energy doing?

The simple, uncomplicated answer was; life was surviving, even though it underwent many changes in form.

The dynamic principle of existence, then, was the primary urge of all organisms, from the lowest unicellular to the most complex, to survive.

In the case of human beings, this will to exist expressed itself in four dynamics or drives. (Hubbard later posited four more, making a total of eight.) The original four were: (1) The urge to survive as a self-aware individual; (2) through his progeny; (3) as the member of a family group, or race; and (4) through mankind and as all mankind.

"If one sagged down towards unsurvival," wrote Hubbard in *Dianetics: The Evolution of a Science*, "one was goaded up the scale towards survival by pain. One was lured ahead by pleasure into survival. There was a graduated scale with one end in death and the other in immortality."[2]

Man's brain acts as a computer, programmed to deal with all situations relating to survival. When functioning properly, it could and would produce the correct answers to problems. However, it did not always function properly. Something happened to make the "optimum brain", which Hubbard had postulated, produce erroneous data. What was it?

During a series of experiments using hypnotism and narco-synthesis as the best tools then available to him, Hubbard had discovered that the basic personality of man was sincere, intelligent and good. Even the fundamental character of hardened criminals that emerged during the trance state was one whose drives were constructive and benevolent.

"Tentatively and cautiously a conclusion was drawn that the optimum brain is the unaberrated brain, that the optimum brain is also the basic personality, that the basic personality, unless organically deranged, was good. If man were basically good, then only a 'black enchantment' could make him evil."[7]

This preliminary conclusion was important because it gave direction to Hubbard's subsequent research. It posed the first in a line of successive and critical questions which led eventually to one of Dianetics' most valuable discoveries.

Moreover, the theory that all men are basically good and that their wrongdoing stemmed from mental aberration, was indeed exciting. If later experiment proved this working hypothesis valid and a means could be found of eliminating the aberrations, it could mean the redemption of mankind – the criminal, the alienated, the anti-social, disruptive, the drug addict, the war-monger.

To this day that broad hope sounds through much of the literature of Scientology, as well as in the day-to-day statements of its founder.

Still using the analogy of a data processing system, Hubbard identified the human computer as the "analytical mind". It was this analyser which sets man apart from all other animals.

Hubbard theorized that aberrative circuits had somehow been introduced into the basically "good" computer from the external world, thus producing error. He illustrated his thesis by comparing the operation of the mind to a common adding machine.

"We put into it the order that all of its solutions must contain the figure 7. We hold down 7 and put on the computer the problem of 6 + 1. The answer is wrong. But we still hold down 7. To all intents and purposes here, that machine is crazy. Why? Because it won't compute accurately so long as seven is held down. Now release 7 and put a very large problem on the machine and get a correct answer. The machine is now sane – rational."

The question still remained: what was holding down figure 7, so to speak, in computations made by the analytical mind?

Further investigation by the use of hypnosis led to the discovery that the source of the trouble lay in a previously unknown sub-mind which, together with its own memory bank, underlies the analytical or so-called "conscious" mind. It is atavistic, that is, a hold-over from an earlier stage of man's evolution. Hubbard called this subliminal mechanism the reactive mind. Far from being the "unconscious" mind described in textbook psychology, the reactive mind is the *only* mind that is always conscious. It records data associated with what is done to the individual, not by him, during periods of unconsciousness, such as those produced by drugs, injury, shock or illness.

For example, if you are hit by a car as you are crossing the street and are knocked unconscious, all that is said and done around you while you lie waiting for the ambulance, will be recorded by the reactive mind. So will the physical pain, even though you are not consciously aware of it at the time.

"Further, every moment of great emotional shock, where loss occasions near unconsciousness, is fully recorded in the reactive mind ... For instance, the death of a loved one brings about a state of near unconsciousness, and everything which is said or done around a person in such a state is recorded and becomes compulsive as part of the reactive mind."[7]

All the combined perceptions recorded during these traumatic episodes create what in Dianetics is called an *engram*. The *Scientology Abridged Dictionary* defines engram as "a mental image picture of an experience containing pain, unconsciousness and a real or fancied threat to survival; it is a recording in the reactive mind of something which actually happened to an individual in the past and which contained pain and unconsciousness".[3]

The high-priority, survival-oriented data of the engram passes directly into a reactive memory bank, without any evaluation by the analyser or conscious mind.

There it remains, unsuspected by and unavailable to the

conscious memory. But when the individual is in a state of reduced awareness – e.g., excessively tired, drunk or ill – sounds and circumstances in his surroundings similar to those associated with the original experience, will restimulate the engram. "Succeeding moments of restimulation, also recorded as pictures, are called *locks*."

When an engramic recording is restimulated, it reduces to a minimum the function of the analytical mind, and takes over control of the individual, causing him to behave irrationally in accord with its commands. At such times, the person may experience a feeling of dullness, slight stupor and confusion, "a sort of dumb, unreasoned and unidentified emotion that seems to stop thought in numbness".[6]

Hubbard's discovery of this function of a sub-mind was an achievement of immense significance. Although ignored or derided by professional psychologists at the time it was first announced, several leading psychiatrists have recently confirmed Hubbard's work, presenting their findings as their own. However, Dianetics was too well established and widely practiced for any doubt to exist about Hubbard having been the first to formulate principles covering the existence and function of the reactive mind.

Perhaps the principal reason that Hubbard succeeded in uncovering the sub-mind where previous researchers had failed was the fact that he was not tied to the official dogma of orthodox schools. He was free to examine what he called wild radicals. Psychiatric literature is full of case histories which point to the presence of hidden, reactive memories in man – latent mental image pictures that are unavailable to waking consciousness. But in every instance, the unusual features of the case, which should have invited deeper study, were inadequately explained away by accepted hypotheses.

For example, there is the well-documented account of an epileptic patient, a near-illiterate, who during a seizure delivered a full funeral oration in scholarly Latin. According to the report, it was an oration he could never before have heard in its entirety, but was put together from snatches previously overheard under similarly abnormal conditions – *that is, during epileptic seizures, when the conscious mind, the sentient analyser was shut down.*

When the patient returned to a normal state, he could remember nothing of his remarkable performance, nor could he understand a word of the Latin text. He also failed to respond to religiously weighted words in a word-association test.

Even more significantly, hypnosis elicited no more information than did questions and tests under normal conditions of wakefulness.[5]

The Dianeticist would understand at once that the Latin words, perfectly recalled by a man who knew no Latin, were data filed in the "red-tab" memory bank of the reactive mind while the analyser was out of circuit – i.e. during the epileptic seizure.

In his early experiments, Hubbard had tried hypnotism, too, in an unsuccessful effort to contact the submind. He wrote:

"When one tried to go to it with hypnotism, or narco-synthesis he was confronted with a patient who simply looked knocked-out, who was unresponsive to everything. As narco-synthesis and hypnotism both savour of sleep, the deeper sleep of the composite whole of all the past knock-outs of a lifetime render the patient entirely insensible even when one was squarely on top of the reactive bank. So this bank remained hidden and unknown."[8]

Instead of probing deeper into the mystery, as Hubbard did, the psychiatrist who reported the case just cited, ignored the perplexing implications and offered the simplistic explanation that it was an "example of disordered memory".

Another important discovery of Dianetics concerning the human mind was that of the ability of the individual to move along a *time track*, to return to any given moment of his life's history, and to relive that experience in full, including all that was heard, seen, smelled, tasted or touched.

Returning is not the same thing as remembering. Memories are highly selective, edited versions of our experiences. They often omit seemingly unimportant details and stress others; modify, revise and distort the content in conformity with bias, or with certain values.

On the other hand, in Dianetic recall, or returning, the immediate percept of an event is veridical – it is a complete and accurate reproduction.

In Dianetic processing, the guidance of an individual back along this time track to earlier moments became an indispensable tool for contacting the engram bank of the reactive mind which is otherwise unavailable.

"Many people," wrote Hubbard, "are held in these moments by some past physical pain to such a degree that they are actually not in present time. When an individual is somewhere on the time-track other than in present time, he can be said to be out of present time. He will be experiencing some of the pain, and will be reacting to the commands of the moment."[9]

A primary goal of Dianetics is to restore the individual to full, present-time self-determination. This is accomplished by directing him back along his personal time track to contact and re-live the moments of emotion, pain, and unconsciousness that, as real or fancied threats to survival, were filed in the "red-tab" memory bank of the reactive mind.

In this way, the hidden recordings or engrams are gradually reduced and eventually refiled as a non-aberrative memory in the conscious-level banks of the analytical mind, where they can no longer produce irrational behaviour and illness.

According to Dianetic theory, the engram bank is the only portion of human memory whose content can be exhausted.

Such processing takes time because engrams do not

occur singly, but in chains. A chain is a succession of incidents along the time track, related to one another by some similarity such as subject, location, people or perception. The average person's reactive mind contains between fifteen and twenty such chains, with about ten to fifteen engrams to the chain.

Moreover, it isn't a matter of dealing with engrams at random, in the order in which they may be contacted while moving back and forth on the time track. It is necessary to find and erase the basic engram, that is, the primary incident to which subsequent engrams along the chain are linked.

Before the basic engram is located and erased, those which follow it on the chain cannot be fully exhausted, although their command value can be reduced. After erasure of the basic engram, those which follow it along the chain can be lifted without difficulty.

The search for the very first incident on the time track (called basic-basic) led to the discovery of prenatal engrams. Hubbard reported that the earliest could occur shortly *before conception*, and that engramic events *during* the prenatal epoch were common.

Such a postulate meant, of course, that engrams were recorded on the cellular level. It was a highly revolutionary concept. As Hubbard himself declared, "No statement as drastic as this – as far beyond previous experience as this – can be accepted readily."[4]

And indeed, it was not readily accepted by the scientific community at the time. However, medical researchers have since published results of their own studies which validate Hubbard's work.

The Dianetic technique for location and erasing, one by one, the hundreds of engrams in the reactive-mind memory bank is comparatively simple. An *auditor* (a person trained to listen carefully to the individual being processed) directs the attention of the "I" back along the time track. As the preclear (the person undergoing therapy) is thus regressed, the accumulated traumatic experiences of the organism are contacted and reduced by repetitive re-experiencing of them.

The auditing session is conducted while the preclear is in a condition of reverie. It is important here to emphasize that this state of reverie is not in any way related to hypnosis. The preclear is conscious throughout the period of processing. It is axiomatic in Dianetics that hypnotism is never to be used in auditing procedures because hypnosis is itself a source of aberration and will only add another engram to the red-tab bank.

To prevent the preclear's receiving a suggestion even inadvertently, the auditor introduces what is called a *canceller*, as soon as the preclear has closed his eyes and entered a state of mental relaxation. The canceller consists of a statement such as this: "Hereafter, when I say the word 'cancelled', everything which I have said to you during this session will be cancelled and will have no effect on you."

At the end of each session, immediately before the preclear is permitted to open his eyes, the auditor will utter the single word, "Cancelled".

The auditor is also careful before ending the session to bring the preclear back to present time. He is first moved forward on the time track to contact a recent pleasant experience. After re-living that event, the auditor tells him: "Now come up to present time."

If the preclear appears confused or unsure, the auditor makes certain that he has in fact returned to present time by asking him to tell the date, or requesting a "flash answer" to the question: "How old are you?" If he gives his correct age, the preclear has returned to present time.

As already indicated, the ultimate goal of Dianetic processing is to delete the contents of the reactive bank, thereby producing a mental stability in the "cleared" individual.

At this point it is necessary to note that the state known as *clear* in the early days of Dianetics is currently referred to as Dianetic release. The reason is that methods of testing the results of Dianetic therapy were not fully adequate at that time. Subsequent experimentation was to reveal that what Dianeticists regarded as "clears" in the 1950s were, in fact, not clears in an accurate and absolute sense at all.

Further investigation was to bring to light higher levels of processing. The expanded system, which would produce even more dramatic results, was called Scientology, a word derived from the Latin *scio* which means knowing, and the Greek λόγος which means the word or outward form by which the inward thought is expressed.

REFERENCE NOTES

1. Arthur Koestler, *The Act of Creation*. London: 1964.
2. L. Ron Hubbard, *Dianetics: The Evolution of a Science*.
3. *Scientology Abridged Dictionary*.
4. L. Ron Hubbard, *Science of Survival*.
5. George A. Talland, *Disorders of Memory and Learning*. London: 1968.
6. U. Keith Gerry, *The Key To Tomorrow*. Johannesburg: 1955.
7. L. Ron Hubbard, *Scientology: The Fundamentals of Thought*.
8. L. Ron Hubbard, *Scientology 8–80: The Discovery and Increase of Life Energy*.
9. L. Ron Hubbard, *The Creation of Human Ability*.

2. *Scientology: Knowing How to Know*

It would be difficult to assign an exact historical date on which Scientology was born and Dianetics receded into the background of Hubbard's continuing research.

In a footnote to his book, *Scientology 8–8008*, first published in 1953, Hubbard wrote:

"Dianetics was an evolutionary step, a tool which had use in arriving at a higher level of knowledge; its use, however, produced slower results and much lower goals. Further, Dianetic processes were limited in that they could not be applied more than a few hundred hours without the reactive mind assuming a very high command level over the analytical mind due to the fact that the reactive mind was being validated continually in the process, whereas the better process was to validate the analytical mind."

All this makes good sense; but there were also other compelling reasons for withdrawing from what might be called organized Dianetics and, after a brief interval of thought and study, making a fresh start, incorporating

Dianetics into the more advanced theories and techniques embodied in Scientology.

In the first place, during the Dianetics "boom" which followed publication of the original textbook, centres for the study and practice of the new mental therapy proliferated across the country so rapidly Hubbard was not able to staff all of them with competent and trustworthy personnel.

Furthermore, a campaign to destroy both Dianetics and its founder was in full swing, directed by certain hidden interests (to be given close scrutiny in later chapters), and aided by hostile or irresponsible members of the mass media.

Even those nearest Hubbard Foundation executives who had been active in the organizational phase of Dianetics from the first were a source of difficulty. They were inclined to view the techniques of Dianetics as a finalized system. Data or results that did not fit neatly into the established pattern they wanted simply to ignore – at least publicly.

For example, there was the question of former lives. Time after time during Dianetic auditing, when preclears had been guided along their time track, they had not stopped at the arbitrary barriers of birth or conception, but had spontaneously returned to incidents which had occurred in prior existences.

To Hubbard, whose ultimate aim was eventually "to contact the often-postulated, but never thoroughly sensed, measured, and experienced human soul", such experiences could not be shrugged off. References to the strange phenomena popped up frequently in his public lectures, and he discussed them at length with associates.

His Foundation's board of trustees felt that reincarnation was a controversial subject which would do great harm to both the reputation and the financial prospects of Dianetics if it were made part of the approved auditing procedure.

"I have been many times requested to omit any reference to these [past deaths and past lives] in the present work or in public," wrote Hubbard, "for fear that a general impression would get out that Dianetics had something to do with

Spiritualism. Further, the view has been many times expressed that in view of the fact that prenatals are so 'controversial', the introduction of past lives and past deaths into Dianetics, even as an experimental investigation, would permit old schools of therapy to persist in their delusion that all is delusion.

"This would hardly be a scientific way of handling a science. A true scientist boldly and fearlessly reports that which he finds."[1] (p. 61)

Trustees of the Hubbard Dianetics Research Foundation did not agree with Hubbard's tell the truth and shame the Devil attitude. In July 1950, the board tried to pass a resolution banning the entire subject of past lives from the official Dianetics publications and public lectures.

As a matter of fact, aside from the medical monopolists of AMA and the closed-shop dogmatists of organized psychology (who would have continued to attack Dianetics no matter what course its experimentation might take), reincarnation as a valid subject for further investigation had a wider acceptance among reputable thinkers than the foundation trustees realized.

Certainly, it was not a startlingly new theory. The doctrine of rebirth appeared in India at a very early date and is referred to in such ancient sacred writings as the *Artharva Veda*, the *Laws of Manu*, the *Bhagavat Gita* and the various Upanishads.

It became a fundamental tenet of Buddhism in the sixth century B.C., and with that faith spread to China, Tibet, Ceylon, Burma, Indo-China and Japan.

It was also taught by the mystery schools of ancient Greece, which no doubt received it from Indian sources. In the area of philosophy, it was an essential element in the works of such eminent thinkers as Pythagoras, Socrates, Plato, Empedocles and Heraclitus.

Among Roman men of learning who gave serious attention to the concept of multiple earthly lives were Cicero, Seneca, Ovid, Virgil and Sallust.

Nor did the belief end with these celebrated names of the remote past. To the impressive roster just cited can be added illustrious personages of modern times, who have embraced the doctrine. They include such diverse figures as philosophers Giordano Bruno, Leibnitz, Hume, Lessing, Schlegel, Fichte, Herder, Schopenhauer and Emerson; poets Shelley, Tennyson, Browning and Whitman; composers Wagner and Mahler; Salvador Dali, Henry Ford, Benjamin Franklin, General George Patton and others.

In one of his greatest poems, *Intimations of Immortality,* Wordsworth – a firm believer in reincarnation, wrote:

> *"Our birth is but a sleep and a forgetting:*
> *The Soul that rises with us, our life's Star*
> *Hath had elsewhere its setting,*
> *And cometh from afar:*
> *Not in entire forgetfulness*
> *And not in utter nakedness,*
> *But trailing clouds of glory do we come . . ."*

(According to both Scientology and Eastern beliefs, the Soul returns to earthly embodiment trailing not only clouds of glory, but also the residual import of actions in former lives. These result-potentials, derived from past causes, are called *Karma* by Hindu and Buddhists and *facsimiles* by Scientologists.)

In his own treatment of the subject, Hubbard proceeded with the caution of a chemist. He expressed the view that some supposed experiences of past lives were in fact fantasies based upon reading and imagination (in which case, there would be no somatics – physical pain and discomfort associated with re-experiencing an event).

At the same time, he said, there were other cases which seemed to be real and valid experiences.

Hubbard classified the theory of rebirth under the heading of Para-Scientology, "that large bin which includes all greater or lesser uncertainties . . . the things of which the common normal observer cannot be sure without a little study".

"However," wrote Hubbard in *Scientology: The Fundamentals of Thought*, "as studies have gone forward, it has become more and more apparent that the senior activity of life is that of the thetan [spirit], and that in the absence of the spirit no further life exists. In the insect kingdom it is not established whether or not each insect is ordered by a spirit or whether one spirit orders enormous numbers of insects."

As regards man, however, Scientology studies found that the individual himself is a spirit controlling a body by means of a mind. This spirit, or thetan can separate from the body without incurring death, and can control a body while thus separated from it.

According to the postulates of Scientology, when the thetan takes leave of his body at death, he does not care to remember the life just lived, hence the veil of forgetfulness that normally conceals from us our former existences. The thetan "cannot actually experience death and counterfeits it by forgetting".

At the same time, "he is very anxious to put something on the 'time track' (something for the future) in order to have something to come back to; thus we have the anxieties of sex. There must be additional bodies for the next life. It is obvious that what we create in our societies during this life-time affects us during our next life-time."

Just as ancient philosophies and religions posited the law of return, that is, of an immortal soul which lives successive lifetimes in different bodies, so they also had as their ultimate goal spiritual liberation. This state of ultimate freedom meant freedom from all material bondage and was called *moksha* by the Hindu schools and *Nirvana* by the Buddhists.

What, then, was new about Scientology, whose stated

goal was also Total Freedom for the deathless being or thetan, who passed from life, through life to life?

According to Hubbard, it was methodology. He freely acknowledged his indebtedness to Eastern thought (especially Buddhism), but noted that while the Oriental systems of self-culture contain truths of the highest order, the ascetic demands made upon their aspirants to freedom are such as to render them impractical for most people. Indeed, you could count on one hand the number of truly illumined yogis and boddhisatvas who have appeared on the human scene during the past two or three millennia.

Scientology, on the other hand, claims to have developed techniques for accomplishing in months the kind of spiritual advancement the Buddhist may spend one or many lifetimes to achieve.

"The essence of Scientology is its practicality: its application is broad and its results are uniformly predictable."[2] (p. 12)

Hubbard thus bases the practice of Scientology squarely upon scientific procedure, even though the results claimed for it go well beyond any objective currently envisioned by the physical sciences.

A key concept in Scientology is that known as Cycle of Action, which is defined as a span of time set up within the timeless universe – during which an action takes place.

For example, we are born, we grow up, mature, age, and die. In abstract terms, this means creation, growth, conservation, decay and death or destruction. It would be the cycle of any object.

But such a cycle of action, according to the precepts of Scientology, is only an *apparency*, something which appears to us as real, but which may be quite different from what we *consider* or postulate it to be. "In Scientology," wrote Hubbard, "it can be seen that none of these steps are necessary. One considers them so and they are 'true'. A man can grow old quickly or slowly. He grows old to the degree that he believes he is growing old. Because everyone agrees that this is the way things are, they go that way. The cycle is not true ... The woman, growing old, wishing to appear younger, is protesting this Cycle of Action. She feels there is something wrong with it. There is. We have to find out what the *actual* cycle is before we can make people better."

The most important difference between the apparent cycle and the actual cycle is that instead of destruction, or death, as in the apparent cycle, in actuality, there is only "creation against creation".

Hubbard illustrates this difference with an example of a standing wall. To be apparent, the wall must be in a constant state of creation. To destroy the wall means to exert against it a counter-creativeness in the action of knocking it down. Both the wall standing and the motion of knocking it down are creative actions. "Because we may object to (argue against, dislike) a wall being knocked down, we vilify (swear at, scorn) the creativeness involved in knocking it down with the word 'destructive'."

In addition to counter-creation, there is another kind of "destruction" which is simply the absence of creation. Continuing with the wall illustration, this means that by no longer being a party to the wall's creation, "the wall, in theory, can cease to exist for one".

Fundamentally, then, the *actual* cycle of action contains nothing but *creation*.

According to Scientology, there are three conditions of existence or component parts of experience. In order of their importance, they are: be, do, have.

To be is to assume some kind of identity. For example, one's name, physical characteristics, titles, ranks, and so on. Yet, "the only true identity is 'myself'. It is not a name, it is not a designation."

The preclear, on the other hand, often assumes, to a greater or lesser extent, the identity of others – that of his father or mother, marital partner, private hero, "or any or all of thousands of possible people".

Hubbard speaks of this living other people's lives as being in their *valence*. Scientology defines valence (a term used by Gestalt psychology in quite a different connotation) as a false identity, with all of its peculiarities and characteristics, assumed unwittingly.

As a mechanism of survival, valence "is used by the mind to escape pain or defeat. In an accident, if the preclear suffered unconsciousness from pain or emotion, he may pick up the valence, or personality, of any of the dramatic personnel involved, whether there was only one other or a dozen."

Another reason that we are inclined to live in the valence of others is that we are "attention-hungry". We look at things outside ourselves and, to balance the flow of our attention, we feel we must also be looked at. We want to get attention.

Since an individual assumes the identity of the person who gets attention, in Scientology processing, the auditor is alert to attempts by the preclear to identify with one or other of his parents. "He got into his father's valence when he found he could get no attention from mother. Observing that the father got some of her attention, he took father's identity. However, let us say he didn't like father. The auditor finds him hating himself. 'Himself' is really father."

Hubbard avowed: "There *is* a basic personality, a person's *own* identity. He colours or drowns it with valences as he loses or wins in life. He can be dug up."

The task of the auditor, then, is to help the preclear reclaim his own beingness.

To do, according to Hubbard, is to create an effect. Another way of stating the same proposition would be that doing is engaged in goal-directed action. Unless one can produce some effect in his world-around, he feels that he cannot command the attention he desires. If an individual is unable to create an effect, he may become aberrated, ill, lazy or careless.

"Criminals or maniacs are people who are frantically attempting to create an effect long after they know they cannot. They cannot then create decent effects, only violent effects. Neither can they work (do) ... An artist stops his work when he believes he can no longer create an effect."

It is axiomatic in Scientology that creation of an effect is the paramount purpose in this universe. There are times, however, when one's security may depend upon being able to create *no* effect. For example, if you have taken cover and are hiding from a homicidal pursuer bent on killing you, you try desperately to create no effect in order that a fatal effect will not be created upon you.

In order to create an effect, the action must be upon or against something. Hence, the necessity of *having* something to act upon or against. Hubbard conceives havingness or ownership as the individual's ability to see, touch or occupy objects.

In that sense, we can possess many things of which we are not the *legal* owners. For example, one can have a valuable painting, even though it is in the physical possession of someone else, merely by seeing it and deriving aesthetic pleasure from contemplating its beauty or technical excellence.

In such an instance, one may even have a greater part of the painting than the owner in whose house it hangs. "Rich and successful men," wrote Hubbard, "have carried ownership to such an extent that they are themselves thoroughly encased in energy which is solidifying into *mest* itself. [*Mest* is an acronym, from *matter, energy, space* and *time* – the ingredients of the physical universe.] Instead of having things, they themselves are had by things." In other words, instead of creating an effect, as was their intention, they have in fact, *become* an effect.

The question of ownership is a crucial one in Scientology

because aberrations to be found in the processing of a preclear were created by a "reversal of havingness", that is, the individual did not want something, but had to have it; or he wanted something and found it impossible to have it; or he wanted one thing and got something else.

"The entire problem of the future," wrote Hubbard, "is the problem of goals. The entire problem of goals is the problem of possession. The entire problem of possession is the problem of time."

Scientology views life as a game – or games – which people play.

This idea in its bare essentials is not new – Hinduism posits the cosmic "play" of the Shakti or Divine Mother. But again, Hubbard develops the concept along new and distinct lines.

First of all, he describes a game as a contest between individuals or teams, consisting of three elements, namely, freedom, barriers and purposes. Purpose, of course, is another word for goal, and the ultimate goal of any game is to outplay the opponent and win.

The warring of inimical purpose between opposing players produces problems. "A problem consists of two or more purposes opposed. It does not matter what problem you face or have faced, the basic anatomy of that problem is purpose-counter-purpose."

Hubbard's concept of freedom balanced by barriers or rules of the game is obviously relevant to such human concerns as ideologies, government, and social mores. He observes that the reason great revolutionary movements always fail is that "they promise unlimited freedom. That is the road to failure. Only stupid visionaries chant of endless freedom. Only the afraid and the ignorant speak of and insist upon unlimited barriers."

In considering freedom, it is necessary to ask: freedom *from* what, freedom to *do* what? "Freedom from" is all right only so long as there is a place to be free *to*. Total freedom would be a freedom without purpose and would end in some kind of dictatorship.

Total barriers also create a no-game condition and must end in failure. A dictator or a self-appointed elite in government, who seek to impose upon the population absolute rule in which there no longer exists any freedom of choice are self-destructive. Sooner or later they will be overthrown. The only justifiable legal barriers a government can set up are laws limiting actions to be injurious or fatal to other members of society.

Hubbard cites three ways in which government can bring about chaos: (1) by seeming to give endless freedom; (2) by seeming to impose endless restraints or barriers; (3) by making neither freedom nor barriers certain.

As this is written, the U.S. government, controlled by pressure groups and vested interests, appears to be practicing all three of these modalities at the same time. In the first instance, official tolerance has spawned chaos and disorder by militants and subversives in American Society, while in the second, an autocratic bureaucracy has intervened in the life of all citizens, to impose restraints upon virtually everything they do. Finally, both the courts and the quasi-legal administrative hearings before federal commissions have made so many discriminatory and contradictory rulings that there is no certainty about either one's freedom nor the laws governing necessary acts.

At this point, it is necessary to recall the dynamics or basic impulses in life, postulated by Scientology. Four of them were cited in the chapter on Dianetics; they were: (1) the urge towards survival as self; (2) the urge towards survival through the sexual act or through the begetting and rearing of children; (3) the urge towards survival through a group of individuals, or as a group; and (4) the urge towards survival through all mankind.

During the development of Scientology, four additional dynamics were discovered, making a total of eight. The final four were: (5) the urge towards survival through all living things, whether animal or vegetable; (6) the urge towards survival as the physical universe or *mest*; (7) the urge towards survival as or of spirits; and (8) the urge towards survival as Infinity, or through a Supreme Being.

One has only to review the scheme of these eight dynamics to see the combination of "teams" possible in playing the various games of existence. "The self dynamic can ally itself with the animal dynamic against, let us say, the universe dynamic and so have a game. In other words, the dynamics are an outline of possible teams and interplays. As everyone is engaged in several games, an examination of the dynamics will plot and clarify for him the various teams he is playing on and those he is playing against. If an individual can discover that he is only playing on the self dynamic and that he belongs to no other team, it is certain that this individual will lose, for he has before him seven remaining dynamics. And the self is seldom capable of bestowing by itself all the remaining dynamics."

Scientology designates this type of game, that is, playing on the first dynamic alone, self-determination.

There is also the situation in which an individual plays or controls both sides of a game in much the same way as a chess player may set up the board and alternately play both sides in order to develop a new strategy. Scientologists call this kind of play *pan-determinism*. "By creating problems, one tends to view both sides in opposition and so becomes pan-determined." For this reason, during Scientology processing, the preclear is sometimes called upon to invent problems which will widen his field of vision and thus exteriorize him from self complication.

There remains one other aspect of Scientology's games of life concept which should be mentioned here. That is the question of the player's volition. If he is forced into a game in which he has no interest or which is repugnant to him, such as the game of fighting a war as an unwilling conscript or of being obliged to become a political partisan in order to find employment, he may eventually fall into a state of apathy or a no-game condition.

Scientology lays great emphasis upon the importance of communication, or interchange of ideas between people. "The ability to communicate is the key to success in life."

In its widest sense, communication embraces the transmitting of data not only from person to person, but from part of the universe to the individual, or from one's own memory recordings to himself. "Communication uses all the physical senses – sight, hearing, touch, smell, taste – as well as the fifty or more perceptics in any and all possible combinations, to relay data to the 'I' or to other organisms."

In human relationships, communication forms one angle of a triangle symbolizing all of life's activities. Hubbard called it the A–R–C triangle, the A standing for Affinity, the R for Reality and the C for Communication.

Affinity is used here to mean any emotional attitude such as loving or liking – the degree of attraction felt by one individual in relation to another. There are many levels of affinity, ranging from love, strong and outgoing at the top of the "tone scale", down through enthusiasm, conservatism, boredom, antagonism, anger, covert hostility, fear, grief and finally to outright apathy. Below apathy, the scale descends deeper and deeper into "solidities such as matter".

Reality, the remaining factor of the A–R–C triad is, in the present context, that upon which people agree as real.

While Communication is the most important angle of the A–R–C, it can readily be seen that without the other two – Affinity and Reality – satisfactory communication is not possible.

The philosopher, George Santayana, once observed that all men readily receive that for which they are prepared, but all else they ignore; or pronounce to be monstrous and wrong; or deny to be possible. "A communication, to be received," wrote Hubbard, "must approximate the affinity level of the person to whom it is directed."

There must be some degree of mutual liking between the person imparting data and the person receiving it. That is why it is difficult if not impossible to communicate with someone who is very angry with you. There must also be some common ground of agreement about so-called facts – that which both parties take for granted. "Without affinity there can be no agreement; without agreement, no communication; and without communication, reality drops to an inoperable low."

Scientology thus seeks to raise an individual from a lower to a higher position on the tone scale, where communication is improved and he experiences love, friendliness and easy discourse with others.

The alternative is not very appealing. As we go lower on the scale, communication between men (and hence between nations) becomes poorer until we reach hatred. Hubbard warns: "Where the affinity level is hate, the agreement is solid matter, and the communications . . . bullets."

According to Scientology, man is a trinity; consisting of spirit, mind and body.

Hubbard once said that the greatest contribution Scientology has made to human knowledge is the isolation, description and handling of the spirit of man. He writes that in 1951, "I established along scientific rather than religious or humanitarian lines, that thing which is the person, the personality; is separable from the body and the mind at will and without causing bodily death or mental derangement."

In order that his own concept of spirit would not be confused with traditional interpretations of that word, Hubbard assigned to it the name *thetan*, from the Greek letter θ, theta – used in mathematical equations. He declared that the thetan is immortal; it possesses no mass, no wave-length, no energy, no time, and no location in space except by broadly agreed-upon considerations.

The thetan is not a thing nor an effect, but the creator of both, as a free and efficient cause. It can exist, as a construct in one of four conditions, viz. wholly separate from a body or even from this universe; near a body, which it consciously controls; within a body, which it animates; or in coerced separation from a body, which he is not permitted to approach or to control (i.e., the inverted state called death).

Of the four situations cited above, Scientology regards the second – that is, being near a body and controlling it – as optimal. "One of the many goals of processing in Scientology is to 'exteriorize' the individual and place him in the second condition above, since it has been discovered that he is happier and more capable when so situated."

According to Hubbard, the thetan, when thus separated from the body, can correct anything that may be wrong with his own body or that of another.

Hubbard makes it quite clear that exteriorization of the spirit or thetan by techniques of Scientology is not the same thing as so-called projection of the astral body, practiced by occultists ."Astral bodies," he wrote, "are usually mock-ups which the mystic then tries to believe real. He sees the astral body as something else and then seeks to inhabit it in the most common practices of 'astral walking'." The projected thetan, on the other hand, does not possess a body (astral or otherwise). The description given by Scientology, in fact, recalls Dr. Andrija Puharich's definition of the "I" or real person as a "nuclear mobile centre of consciousness".

The human mind is the mechanism which the thetan uses to control the body and to communicate with his physical environment. "The thetan receives, by the communication system called the mind, various impressions, including direct views of the physical universe."

In addition to the analytical, reactive and somatic minds mentioned earlier in our discussion of Dianetics, the thetan has access to other sources of knowledge and, Hubbard asserts, is himself close to a total knowingness. Existing outside of time, he knows not only things of the past, but also those of the future that are unrelated to present stimuli or to data stored in the analytical and reactive memory banks.

The third part of man – the physical body – Hubbard once described in engineering terms as a carbon-oxygen engine which operates at a temperature of 98.6 degrees Farenheit on low-combustion fuel, generally derived from other life forms.

Later, various experiments led to the discovery of more subtle functions in and around the physical body. One of the most important of these was a fixed electrical field surrounding the body. Although wholly independent of the mind, this field could be influenced by mind, that is, by the thetan acting through the mind.

Recent experiments by Dr. Robert O. Becker, an orthopaedic surgeon at Syracuse Veterans Administration Hospital (and others) have confirmed Hubbard's postulate that a bioelectric field envelops the body.

According to Hubbard, this electric field monitors the physical structure of the body and can alter its physical characteristics or modify its inter-related functions.

Obviously referring to treatments still employed by orthodox psychiatry, he warns that "the use of electrical shocks upon a body for any purpose is therefore very dangerous and is not condoned by sensible men. Of course, the use of electric shock was never intended to be therapeutic but was intended only to bring about obedience by duress, and, as far as it can be discovered, to make the entirety of insanity a horror."

Hubbard asserts that electrical shock is always followed by bad health and only shortens the life of the patient forced to undergo such brutal interventions. He accuses psychiatrists who use such therapies of practicing "partial euthanasia".

Intimately associated with the tripartite make-up of man is the question of *control*. In the course of his discussion of the human trinity, Hubbard notes that in Scientology, control is defined as start, change and stop, which "can be graphed alongside the apparent cycle of action – create, survive, destroy".

Mental abnormalities of various kinds all stem from the individual's inability to start, to change or to stop. States of apathy or of hysterical paralysis occur when a person is unable to start anything; a fixation neurosis is the result of being unable to change something; and compulsive behaviour in which an action, habit, belief, etc. is carried beyond the limits of common sense, arises from the inability to stop.

"An individual who has a free heart and mind about life is bent upon creating [i.e., starting] things."

In "playing the game" of existence, according to Scientology, the thetan himself creates the physical universe (MEST) and initiates activity within that world. However, the thetan can lose effective control of the activities he has started by becoming too self-involved with his own creation, thereby losing pandeterminism.

"If a thetan can suffer from anything, it is being out-created (created against too thoroughly). The manifestations of being out-created would be destruction of his own creations and the overpowering presence of other creations. Thus, a thetan can be brought to believe that he is trapped if he is out-created."

This loss of control by the thetan is passed on to the mind, which then suffers the same inability to start, change or stop; and from the mind it is passed on to the body, which suffers similar inabilities.

In a strict sense, of course, these problems are only apparent (the Buddhist likens them to "a tiger in a dream") since they are difficulties of consideration, or as Hubbard put it: "as the thetan considers, so he is".

A major goal of Scientology is to restore to the thetan the control he has lost. Freed of aberrations and with improved capability, he can then "play the game" with a better chance of wins.

Central to this effective application of Scientology are procedures which, while similar in many respects to the earlier practice of Dianetic auditing, are broader in scan and more varied in their ultimate purposes.

For example, the role of the Dianetic auditor was to listen and to compute. In addition to these two functions, the auditor in Scientology also guides the preclear. This means, essentially, that he conducts the preclear through certain routines, some verbal and others requiring the use of common objects in the auditing room, all aimed at what Hubbard terms "establishing game conditions".

It lies outside the scope of this book to present detailed descriptions of the various drills and techniques involved in Scientology processing. Suffice it to say that, generally speaking, where Dianetic auditing sought to "clear" the individual by locating and running specific engrams one by one, beginning with the basic engram, Scientology's *modus operandi* is addressed directly to the thetan or soul and, by assisting him to raise his level of awareness, erases the engrams without dealing with them directly and singly.

Among other benefits claimed for Scientology's processing are a higher IQ; increased ability to communicate; greater domestic harmony; improvement in health, social attitudes and artistic creativity.

(An over-all picture of the various factors dealt with may be gained by examining the Hubbard Chart of Human Evaluation. Processing seeks to raise the preclear's level in each and all of the categories represented on the chart).

To sum up:

Scientology is an applied religious philosophy which

conceives man as a triad – body, mind and soul (or thetan).

Although he is by nature basically good, man indulges in aberrative or evil behaviour because of painful past experiences stored in the memory bank of his reactive mind (once called the subconscious) and in the thetan's own record of experiences in former lives.

The basic urge of man and indeed of all organic life, is that of *survival*. In the case of the human, that urge expresses itself in one or more of eight dynamics: self, sex and family, groups, mankind, life forms, the physical universe, the spiritual universe and the Supreme Being.

According to Hubbard, all life is an interplay between statics and kinetics. The static of Scientology is not quite the same as the theory in physics known by the same term. In physics, static is represented by bodies or forces at rest or in equilibrium. But, Hubbard points out, a material body at rest is itself in motion, if only on the level of molecular motion.

On the other hand, Scientology posits a static, designated by the mathematical symbol θ that is wholly motionless. It has no mass, no motion, no wavelength and no location in space or in time.

The thetan, while existing as true static, is an "awareness of awareness unit", capable of formulating considerations, and possessing the ability to postulate and to perceive.

The opposite of motionless theta or static, is all-motion kinetics, called MEST, that word being formed from the first letters of the elements constituting kinetics: matter, energy, space and time.

The cycle of action through which the material universe moves is: create, survive and destroy.

"The interplay between theta and MEST results in activities known as life, and causes the animation of living life forms." This means that each thetan creates his world and that reality is the broadly agreed upon considerations of the community of soul or thetans, who play the game of life.

In reply to my question, what is the relation of God to the community of souls, the Rev. Robert H. Thomas, leading authority on Scientology in the U.S., said: "This is left up to the intuition of each individual. He finds it out for himself. I can give you my personal viewpoint. God, I think, is to be considered infinite potential. But the infinite potential is a senior concept to any individual manifestation of it. The individual manifestation contains and in some ways expresses and manifests that infinite potentiality. If you view yourself as the total, then you are the total. If you view yourself as the individual, you are the individual. The conditions of limitation and temporality are imposed by the viewpoint. But inherent in the viewpoint is the potentiality.

"Essentially, what we consider is that the static – or Theta defined as Static – is senior to any particularity of data. Therefore, the qualitative essence of the Creator cannot be described or qualified in terms of the created objects. That's one of the basic sources of a paradox.

"The multiplicity of viewpoints among the community of Souls is an artificial division which is just junior to integration. It isn't either integration or division. Each individual, discreet being steps into and out of the game.

"At the apex of this gradient scale of universal forms, you have the coexistence of static viewpoints. Then gradually the viewpoints break apart – more and more apart – and you have the creation of the physical universe and its energy manifestations, with the separateness of each viewpoint more and more solidified and enforced by the unwillingness to take responsibility for creating.

"We know, of course, that matter and energy are interchangeable; but in gross apparency, they are distinct. If you think of matter as mental-image pictures, as a basically more refined state of MEST, dreams become just a finer degree of, but at the same time, quantitatively, as the practical, external structure of the universe.

"To rehabilitate the individual thetan to his full omniscient and omnipotent capability of creating universes, it is necessary only to follow the line of rehabilitating his ability to create mental-image pictures. Because, we're postulating that these mental-image pictures and the seeming solidity of the physical universe are one and the same."

This concept of the universe as the embodiment of psycho-mental energy patterns produced by the thetan, closely parallels one held by Tibetan Tantrism. I summarized the Eastern viewpoint in a work on the subject, written several years ago: "As the Tantrik conceives it, mind is the noumenal source of all phenomena. All aspects of creation, regardless of how tangible and objective they may seem to be in the physical world, are only thought images projected by God or by other entities."

Another fundamental idea in Scientology is that of the A–R–C triangle representing the three interdependent components of understanding: affinity, reality and communication. There, affinity means love or degree of liking; reality is that which is agreed upon between thetans; and communication is the interchange of ideas between two or more individuals. Most important of these three is communication. Only by recovering his ability to communicate can the thetan resolve the problems of his life and move towards the ultimate goal of total knowingness, which "would consist of total A–R–C".

Scientology has developed various drills and exercises used in auditing processes, all aimed at helping the thetan solve the problems of the thetan as MEST. "To solve any problem, it is only necessary to become theta the solver, rather than theta the problem." He is then "at cause", and his objective is to be totally at cause, which means being totally free.

Such, in greatly abridged form, are the fundamental principles of Scientology. As a generalized summary, it is open to criticism on a number of accounts. However, as stated in the preface, the present work is not meant to be a complete and authoritative exposition of Scientology. Those who wish a more extensive knowledge of the subject will find it in the writings of L. Ron Hubbard himself, available at Scientology centres throughout the world.

Many seminal ideas derived from Hubbard's work have now obtained broad acceptance without being acknowledged as originating with him.

First and foremost of these is the Scientology postulate that man possesses a sub-mind which remains always alert and retains accurate memories of a traumatic experience such as an operation, even though the conscious (or analytical) mind has temporarily ceased to function (for example, owing to anaesthesia in the case of surgery).

When Hubbard first published his work on Dianetics in 1950, in which he presented this concept in considerable detail, the media were derisive and hostile. Twelve years later, when a San Francisco surgeon announced his "discovery" of the same thing, the press treated his statements with great respect, even though some of them closely paralleled the earlier assertions made by Hubbard.

"One surgeon," said the news account, "believes there no longer can be the slightest doubt that the fully anaesthetized surgical patient can both hear and remember what he hears even though he is unconscious.

"For that reason, the surgeon warned his fellow surgeons and their nurses that they had better start being careful about what they say to one another while working in the operating room.

"Dr. David B. Cheek, San Francisco, a fellow of the American College of Surgeons, relied largely on evidence produced by hypnosis and psychoanalysis. The evidence is now voluminous enough to be conclusive," he said.

Dr. Cheek noted in the interview that technical conversations overheard by the patient while he was in an "unconscious" state could cause surgical shock and changes in body functions, endangering the surgical outcome.

"Anaesthetized persons," he said, "are in a state resembling that of persons in deep hypnotic trance. They're highly suggestible," he went on, "but unhappily the subconscious mind operates on an infantile level and what it hears and deals with while the conscious mind is knocked out by the anaesthesia can be highly disturbing.

"Statements which would otherwise be innocuous may become powerfully dangerous. The remark, 'This thing isn't working', may apply to the suction apparatus, but may fill the anaesthetized patient with fears about his anatomy."

A Scientologist who read the story in his newspaper wrote to Dr. Cheek, directing his attention to the similarity of his statements to the studies reported by Hubbard more than a decade previously.

In reply, Dr. Cheek said; "I am well acquainted with the work of Mr. Hubbard, and agree that there is much in his teaching that has been excellent.

"I am not claiming that I am the first to have sensed that unconscious people pick up unconscious thoughts. I believe James Braid (1795–1860) tried unsuccessfully to see whether anaesthetized patients could hear. Dave Elman has told me in a personal communication that in 1948 he had the experience of being asked to work with a patient who was vomiting after a gall bladder operation. Accidentally, he said, he found that the patient reported verbatim a remark made by the surgeon that had been misunderstood. Correction of this misunderstanding enabled the patient to start eating and recover rapidly."

During one of my conversations with Bob Thomas at Scientology's Los Angeles headquarters, he mentioned that in the late 1950s, Scientologists developed a certain type of training routine, which became the precursor of what one school of psychologists have now popularized as "sensitivity training".

"It's actually an undisciplined distortion of what we originally experimented with. I know for a fact that Dr. William Schutz, who's one of the exemplars of this movement, used Scientology processes in special training. He wrote a book called *Joy: Expanding Human Awareness.*

"In a very early book on Dianetics by Dr. J. A. Winter, there's an introduction by the famous psychologist, Dr. Fritz Pearls, who says that he has used some of Hubbard's technology – namely, repeater technology, which is simply repeating phrases that the patient might come up with, repeating them and going back into the traumatic experience, using the repeated phrases as a lead-in. He found that quite workable."

Time magazine, a consistently biased critic of Hubbard and his work had to credit the founder of Dianetics (in a characteristic left-handed way) with being the first to publish data concerning prenatal memory, when the theory came to be accepted in orthodox professional circles. In the medical department of the magazine's June 8, 1953 issue, an article reported that "Up to now, most psychiatrists have been content to stop their dredging of the past at early childhood. They have left to Dianetician L. Ron Hubbard the primordial darkness extending back from birth to conception and still further back to such matters as 'memory' of life on other planets. Now a serious British phychiatrist, who conducts much analysis under hypnosis, seriously claims to have dredged his patients' memories back to the womb. And though Dr. Denys E. R. Kelsey's report and conclusions seem fantastic to the layman, London's reputable *Journal of Mental Science* prints them with a straight face."

After citing three of the case histories reported by Dr. Kelsey, *Time* quoted him as saying: "It is my belief that these so-called fantasies are in fact the reliving of events which were experienced and appreciated and promptly repressed."

Not long ago, an American psychologist elbowed his way on to the front pages of newspapers across the country with the announcement that "the minds of many individuals can leave their bodies and drift away, uninhibited by physical barriers or distance".

Dr. E. E. Barnard, the psychologist whose statements were released over the wires of Associated Press, described the phenomenon as "like lying on a sofa, getting up and seeing your body still lying on the couch". He insisted that such experiences were not hallucinations and emphasized that his research had known that such "mind projection" causes no harm to the individual.

"I believe," he said, "that man has the ability to perform this phenomenon. If he can be taught to project and control, the prospects are staggering."

Was Dr. Barnard indeed unaware that Scientology textbooks published long before his "discovery" contain step-by-step procedures for both projection and out-of-the-body control? It is hard to resist the suspicion that at some date in the not too distant future the Hubbard methodology will emerge (in suitably modified form) as a sequel to the announcement of Dr. Bernard's initial studies.

Even Hubbard's findings that effective processing of the thetan must deal with stored facsimiles of past lives seems destined to be re-discovered by the orthodox schools of psychology and medicine.

In its February 13, 1969 issue, the *London Sketch* reviewed a book entitled *Many Lifetimes*, co-authored by an English psychiatrist and his wife, that provides "earnest, unsensational evidence" that some of the author's patients not only recalled prior lives, but upon becoming aware of them and reliving some traumatic experiences suffered at that time, were relieved of various neuroses, alcoholism, homosexuality, and so on.

The psychiatrist concluded that many symptoms exhibited by patients, which psychiatry has not been able to treat successfully, have their roots in former lives of the patients. He suggests that such illnesses could well be handled by a look at earlier existences.

Hubbard had thoroughly explored this area of psychiatry's *terra incognita* fully ten years before, and had published detailed reports of his research. One of his books, *Have You Lived Before This Life?* includes seventy case histories of persons who, during Scientology processing showed evidence of having lived before.

REFERENCE NOTES

1. George Bernard Shaw, *Doctors' Delusions*, London: 1950.
2. L. Ron Hubbard, *Dianetics: The Modern Science of Mental Health*.

3. *The Hubbard Electrometer*

There is one other feature of Scientology processing which merits our close attention because of the important role it has played in the official persecution of Scientologists, especially in America.

That is use of the device known as the Hubbard Electrometer or E-meter.

Technically, the instrument is a highly refined type of Wheatstone Bridge – an electronic device used to measure the resistance (in units called "ohms") to a flow of electrical current passing through it.

The Hubbard version of the E-meter (Mark V) has been specially designed to measure both large and minute changes, regardless of how quickly they occur, in the resistance of the human body to a very low-voltage current of electricity. The instrument contains transistorized, printed circuitry, connected to a galvanometer which indicates the amount of resistance offered by a body connected between two electrodes attached to either side of the device.

The display panel is equipped with an on-off switch, a "tone-arm", and three knobs for adjusting the instrument's sensitivity, for changing the calibration and for varying the range. Re-chargeable batteries provide power for the meter's operation.

During processing, the preclear grips two tin cans, one in each hand, attached to the electrode lead wires.

The dial and the control panel of the instrument face the auditor, usually out of view of the person being audited. As the pc responds to questions or reacts to mental stimulus, the auditor observes the action of the needle on the ohm-meter dial. According to Scientology theory, based on extensive tests made with the instrument, the individual's emotional state instantly causes an increase or a decrease in his body's resistance to the small trickle of electricity being passed through him. In the book, *E-Meter Essentials*, Hubbard says: "This current is influenced by the mental masses, pictures, circuits and machinery. When the unclear pc thinks of something, these mental items shift and this registers on the meter."

There are ten principal kinds of needle activity that are considered indicative in auditing. These are: the *stuck* needle (no movement); *fall* (movement to the right); *rise* (movement to the left); *theta bop* (steady dance of the needle); *rock slam* (when needle back and forth in unequal jerky motion); *stage four* (needle goes up an inch or two, sticks, falls and repeats this action;) *floating* (when the needle floats free over a wide area, unaffected by questions or commands); *nul* (when needle is active on its own, but uninfluenced by auditing questions); *change of characteristic* and *body reactions*.

Scientologists regard the E-meter as an indispensable auditing tool when employed by an auditor thoroughly trained in its operation. They say it answers a long-felt need for scientific accuracy in measuring "the impingement of the individual himself upon the body by the direct action of thought".

To prove that the E-meter does, in fact, measure the intensity of facsimiles or mental-image pictures of past incidents, Scientologists often invite the preclear to participate in a simple test. Hubbard gives the following instructions for the demonstration:

"Place the electrodes in the hands of a person. Then pinch that person. You will see the needle of the E-meter duck. Now tell the person to go back to the moment you pinched him and 'feel the pinch again'. He will do so and you will see that the needle ducks just as it did when you first pinched him. In other words, you made a facsimile containing pain when you pinched him. Now you command the facsimile to come back. You see it read again on the meter just as it did when you pinched him. If you make him go through the pinch several times, you will find the needle action grows less and less. This, in essence, is a primary principle in Dianetics: that facsimiles exist. It is a prime factor in Dianetic processing that facsimiles can be reduced in intensity."

The auditor does not read the E-meter to detect untruthful answers or lies that the preclear might tell, but only as a measurement of stress. "And stress is what the auditor is trying to find. For stress is the thing which makes the pc ill and aberrated."

According to Hubbard, an experienced auditor can size up the type of person he is dealing with even before the preclear takes the electrodes into his hands. Various attitudes and comments beforehand will give him away. For example:

"If the pc invalidates the instrument, says, 'Oh, one of them things. I hear as how they ain't regular', the auditor knows he is dealing with a case he will have to use a dredge on to find bottom. For this character sees in the E-meter something which is going to 'find him out', something he cannot cheat and lie around, something which will locate and bring sunlight into the dark caverns of his loathsome and horrendous guilt. In this E-meter he sees a tattle-tale which will expose his extra-curricular activities on the second dynamic, his masturbation at the age of one and the real reason dogs hate him, why he shoots ducks and committed grand larceny in college and makes improper proposals in the little boy's room. He doesn't spell it E-meter, he spells it Enemy. And when put on the instrument, he will usually register almost 'off the bottom'; that is to say, the range expander will be over at minus, the tone handle so low the light flickers, and the sensitivity knob so shut down that when asked about the time he murdered his mother, the auditor has to have a magnifying glass to see if the needle moved."

Bob Thomas, senior executive of the Church of Scientology in the United States, described the E-meter as "a confessional aid in Scientology processing".

"The things that people think that other people can't confront listening to or hearing about them are always the first impediments to a complete communication, interpersonal communication between two people; and this kind of communication is an indispensable pre-requisite to any kind of deep, meditative examination. And, of course, those things have to be gotten out of the way. But that is not the total objective of what we think of as the confessional. Our idea of the confessional is the total self-examination of the enlightened spirit.

"Such an examination implies that the barriers that are normally present that prevent such an examination will be removed. We have found that to dissipate those barriers requires a disciplined approach, a routine, a standardized, introspective methodology. Preliminarily, the individual cannot do it by himself, but there are stages of an advanced nature where he does begin to do it by himself.

"The immediate goal of the E-meter is to enhance communication. In other words, just take a parallel: if an analyst were allowing his patient to free-associate, and the patient were connected in some way with a galvanometer which showed the analyst what things the patient mentioned were emotionally charged and what things were not emotionally charged, a lot of time would be saved. So it's simply an assist for the practitioner to direct the individual to areas which he himself may not realize are troubled or charged with emotion or are repressed; and to better direct his attention into those areas, in a very selective way, and in a gradient way – the easiest things first, and the deeper and more difficult confrontations succeeding.

"The E-meter is used throughout Scientology processing, but there are certain processes at certain stages which do not require an E-meter; e.g., directing the person's attention to the environment – what we call objective processing – simply to familiarize himself with his environment. Sometimes people get too introspective and then interiorize; sometimes they need a kind of vacation from themselves. So we have procedures which simply externalize their attention temporarily so they can re-focus their attention to the interior with a renewed vigor. Those kinds of processes don't require the E-meter.

"When the student audits himself, it is called solo auditing. There are one-handed electrodes – where you have two electrodes connected and it can be held in one hand, so they can write and manipulate the dials with the other hand, but that is a very advanced stage of auditing.

"The E-meter is a simple psycho-galvanometer. It's got some increased sensitivity built into it and the myological reactions that you sometimes get in the galvanometer have been damped out by the circuitry, so that the mental reactions, the reactions of the spirit, on the body are emphasized and can be read more clearly. But that's simply the design of the circuitry; it doesn't basically affect the kind of device.

"It registers what is called, commonly, the psycho-galvanomic reflex, which is a reflex that is a poorly understood mechanism of the psyche. The body resistance seems to vary when the individual thinks of a painful or pain-associated or traumatic-associated concept, or word or idea.

This can be by self-stimulation or by external stimulation; by reading a list of words, for example. There are certain words that will be charged and will have significance for the individual that he isn't immediately aware of. And if you ask him about those words, you'll find he will very quickly get into some traumatic area.

"Some very early work on this was done by Jung, who used a list of words. I think he combined it with the psycho-galvanometer. By this word association, he was attempting to increase the effectiveness of the free association techniques, which he was not sure about. Of course, our orientation is not exactly psychotherapeutic because of the total background emphasis we are putting on the enquiry, which is essentially spiritual. What we have essentially is a physical-universe aid to communication. It aids the minister communicating to the parishioner. It's to both their benefits because it enhances the degree and intensity and directness of the communication.

"We have very sophisticated listing processes, in which we ask a general question and get the person to give us a long list of answers. Then we assess that list with the meter. We find out which of those answers gives the largest read and we go in with that as a topic."

Hubbard relates that in the early days of Dianetic auditing, by keeping his fingers on the pulse of the preclear during auditing, he was "crudely and unsatisfactorily" able to detect a reaction when his questions were leading to a heavily charged incident.

Then, during a series of lectures which he gave in California in 1950, an inventor and electronics expert named Volney G. Mathison heard Hubbard mention the problem and set to work constructing an instrument which would be capable, as Hubbard put it, "of measuring the rapid shifts in density of a body under the influence of thought and measuring them well enough to give an auditor a deep and marvelous insight into the mind of his preclear".

This first device was known as the Mathison Electropsycho-meter. During the ensuing years, the instrument was refined and modified through several generations and in accordance with data provided by continuing research. The literature states that the present E-meter is fabricated and assembled according to Hubbard's exact specifications. To ensure that manufacturing standards are maintained, from time to time he random checks the devices being marketed, against the prototype which he keeps in a safe.

Critics of Scientology have sought to discredit the E-meter by asserting that the varied readings are not measurements of emotional states as claimed, but are due to such factors as quantity and salinity of sweat on the palms, area of contact, force of the preclear's grip on the terminals, and variations in the electrical resistance of his skin.

That such is not the case may easily be demonstrated by a number of simple tests, including that cited above, in which the preclear recalls the experience of being pinched.

In connection with our present inquiry, there is another observation to be made regarding the E-meter. It is that the device is harmless, even in the hands of a person ignorant of its proper purpose and operation.

4. *AMA's Operation Catspaw*

The most important fact to keep in mind during any discussion of the American Medical Association is that that organization is a tightly controlled trade union. Its physician members are operating on what Scientologists call the Third Dynamic – survival as a group.

Nothing, of course, is more distasteful to the medical syndicalists than to be reminded of this unpleasant truth. Individually and collectively, they indignantly reject the notion that their profession is characterized by anything less than selfless dedication to those noble principles embodied in the Hippocratic oath.

Organized medicine has spent and continues to spend huge sums to perpetuate the myth that when the AMA defames and persecutes non-union practitioners and unorthodox therapies, it is only to protect the public from the murderous and unskilled hands of quacks and "doorbell doctors".

If this were true, we could only accept their interventions on our behalf with gratitude.

It is not true. Careful observation reveals that their basic motivation is self protectionism. They are moved by the same considerations that prompt the brotherhood of plasterers to denounce cellulose wall boards, or the electricians union to warn against the dangers of having an unlicensed contractor wire your house.

In short, the pious pleadings with which they justify the most ruthless suppression of all therapies that lie outside the pale, are in reality trade arguments.

Such closed-shop practices, when applied to so vital a sector of society as that of the healing arts can have grave consequences.

It can mean, for example, that thousands may have to endure needless suffering and early death because the discovery of a cure or alleviating medication for their disease, made by some gifted individual outside the medical profession, was unavailable to them.

The vast expenditure of both privately donated and public funds for medical research has made it all the more imperative for the medical trade unionists to maintain their grip on every activity related to their profession. To do this, they can, where necessary, enlist the police powers of the government.

In America, the situation is ten times as bad as it is in Britain, where the law does not, with the exception of cancer and venereal disease, forbid the practice of medicine or even of surgery by persons who possess no medical degree. The unregistered (that is, unlicensed) practitioner is, of course, at a great disadvantage in many ways. He cannot prescribe nor possess dangerous drugs, nor use any title which might imply that he is a legally recognized physician; and he is not allowed to sue his clients for non-payment of fees. But he can advise and treat any patient who wishes to consult him.

In America, under similar circumstances, AMA propagandists would immediately warn that unless this *laissez faire* were instantly curbed, a quack who had taken a mail-order course in brain surgery would be wreaking havoc with the population. This merely shows the arrogant contempt they have for the intelligence of the average American.

The British subject still has some freedom of choice, even though that choice is partly invalidated by the fact that if one calls in an unregistered healer to treat a family member or friend, and the patient dies, one can be prosecuted for criminal neglect.

In the United States, however, you can be legally prosecuted for giving your neighbour aspirin or selling him vitamins. People have actually been sent to prison for vending honey, herb teas and harmless mineral mixtures.

One of the reasons that the medical syndicalists could come to exercise such dictatorial authority over us, is the naive and wholly unfounded belief people have in their knowledge and importance. The public attitude towards orthodox practitioners in America amounts to medical idolatry.

Little wonder. We have been told over and over – in force-fed news stories, subsidized books and magazine articles, and in agitprop forums called quackery congresses – that the orthodox physician is the only accept-able person to treat disease or give advice.

Nor are Americans alone in their over-credulous reliance upon medical doctors to perform miracles of healing. Replying to an invitation by the *Manchester Guardian* to write a series of articles, the late Bernard Shaw answered the question, "Have we lost faith?" with the simple sen-tence: "Certainly not; but we have transferred it from God to the General Medical Council."

Shaw described the British public's attitude toward the medical profession as an infatuation as gross as any of those recorded of the witch-doctor ridden tribes of Africa.

"We believe doctors to have miraculous powers, recon-dite knowledge, and divine wisdom. Now the fact is that they have no more miraculous powers than any other skilled workers has. They have no knowledge that is out of the reach of any layman who cares to acquire it; in fact, it may be doubted whether two percent of our general practitioners know as much science as an average lay frequenter of the Royal Institution or University Extension lectures."

There is adequate evidence, both in Britain and elsewhere, to confirm Shaw's assertion that state-established medicine does not possess the infallibility that its omnipotence would suggest. In the United States, according to one writer who painstakingly researched the subject, statistics drawn from their own literature bear witness to the shocking incompetence that exists among the profession. These reports indicate that an estimated 200,000 deaths each year are iatrogenic, that is, caused by doctors. As the writer observes, such a figure makes physicians "a close rival of cancer and heart disease as a major killer of man".

The point to be made here is not that the profession of medicine is irremediably evil and ought to be eradicated with the same brutal thoroughness with which its inquisitors deal with anything threatening professional trade interests. Most thoughtful readers will agree that an honest, dedicated physician (when you can find one) is one of the greatest benefactors human society can have. Oftener than not he is soon hounded out of the profession or actually made to defend himself against criminal charges as is the case of Dr. Andrew Ivy.

No, the question being raised here, and one which should be constantly kept in mind during the discussion which follows, is simply this:

Can a profession whose growing wealth and power depend not upon the people's health, but upon their sickness, be safely entrusted with the awesome authority to bind and to loose in all matters pertaining to the healing arts, medical research, self-treatment, nutrition, mental illness and even spiritual beliefs?

Alert watchdogs of the AMA began sniffing at Dianetics almost from the moment it first appeared in public.

Dianetics: The Modern Science of Mental Health was published in May 1950. Within weeks, AMA strategists began secretly laying the groundwork for a full-scale attack on the new and uncanonical therapy.

As already noted, the book carried an enthusiastic introduction by J. A. Winter, M.D., a practising physician of St. Joseph, Michigan.

The AMA hierarchy reacted to Dr. Winter's lending his name to Dianetics in the same way officials of the Electrical Workers Union would react to one of their members endorsing or avocating a right-to-work law.

The first step was to determine whether Dr. Winter's credentials were, in fact, beyond question. In other words, was he a member in good standing of AMA? A check of the Association's biographic records showed that he was. A graduate of the Marquette University School of Medicine, he was licensed to practise medicine in Michigan and later in New Jersey. Further, he was also a Fellow of the American Medical Association and a member of the Association for the Study of Internal Secretions.

Obviously, the problem of Dr. Winter would have to be handled discreetly behind the scenes, employing those intramural methods of persuasion best known to that part of AMA's official staff charged with insuring compliance. (In England, Dr. Winter would have been struck off the register "for infamous professional conduct".)

As for L. Ron Hubbard and his system of mental therapy called Dianetics – that was another matter. Not only had Hubbard, a non-professional outsider (and therefore a quack), dared to trespass upon a legally restricted area, but his new formula had captivated the public's imagination and threatened to show certified psychiatrists in a bad light. For in his book, Hubbard had minced no words in referring to some of the barbaric practices that still form an integral part of psychiatric procedures. He had written:

"There are probably thousands of ways to get into trouble with mental healing, but all these ways can be classed in these groups: (1) use of shock or surgery on the brain; (2) use of strong drugs; (3) use of hypnosis as such; and (4) trying to cross-breed Dianetics with older forms of therapy."

In order to launch an effective attack on Dianetics, its AMA adversaries needed some authoritative statements by prominent medical men, explaining to the layman why Dianetics was not only quackery, but very dangerous quackery.

Accordingly, Dr. Austin Smith, then editor of the *Journal of the American Medical Association*, on June 1, 1950 sent letters to a number of doctors and medical societies, asking their help. Laymen not privy to the inside workings of the AMA apparatus, will find them enlightening, if somewhat wanting in factual accuracy. For example, in a letter to Dr. Smith, dated June 5, 1950, Theodore Wiprud, executive secretary of the Medical Society of the District of Columbia wrote:

"Upon receipt of your letter of June 1, I got in touch with several physicians who I thought would have some information about L. Ron Hubbard and his book, *Dianetics*. One of them was Captain George N. Raines, Chief of Psychiatry, Naval Medical Center, Bethesda. He does not want to be quoted but told me that Hubbard and Dr. Joseph A. Winter, who, I understand, is a physician licensed in New Jersey, are 'phonies'.

"One of the bases for 'Dianetics' is the premise that the individual, if prompted by semi-hypnosis, can recall intra-uterine experiences and conversations between father and mother within three months after conception. That would be enough to stop anyone but an ignoramus in his tracks, but I am told that some psychiatrists have been intrigued by the idea. At any rate, among the best psychiatrists this is nothing but the bunk."

In another letter replying to Dr. Smith's initiative, Dr. H. Houston Merritt, director of neurological service at New York's Columbia Presbyterian Medical Center, adopted the condescending, slightly derisive tone to be expected of an AMA-member in dealing with anything so "bizarre and unscientific" (his terms) as Dianetics.

"In reply to your letter of June 1," he wrote, "first I beg to advise that I have had no personal experience with Dianetics. Information I have obtained, however, would indicate that this term was coined to describe a 'new' development in the field of psychiatry which uses a philosophical approach combining some of the principles of psychoanalysis, philosophy of Will Durant and the mathematics of the cybernetics school."

Even with these scientific shortcomings, it was inconceivable to Dr. Merritt that a mere layman could have evolved Dianetics. "It is the impression," he continued, "that Hubbard is the ghost writer for Winter. My information in regard to Winter, which may or may not be authentic, indicates that he lives in New Jersey and that he does not have a licence to practice in the State, nor is he a member of the American Medical Association."

(The reader will recall that Dr. Winter *was* licensed to practice in New Jersey and *was* a member in good standing of the AMA.)

Dr. Smith did not go at his undertaking half-heartedly. In addition to writing to various eminent doctors of his acquaintance, he sent a memorandum to Oliver Field, director of AMA's Bureau of Investigation. The note, dated June 5, 1950, suggested that the medical CIA ought to "look into" Dianetics and concluded with the statement that Hubbard "is alleged to be a 'bad actor, a kind of faker or even worse', but this is not for quoting until more facts are obtained".

Dr. Smith also wrote to another AMA member, Dr. Erwin E. Nelson, then director of the federal Food and Drug Administration.

As I have pointed out elsewhere, from the time of its inception to the present day, FDA has maintained a cozy liaison with AMA. Most of the top decision makers in the federal agency are members of AMA. It hardly seems strange, therefore, that in the past the FDA attitude most often has been (in matters of concern to AMA) that what is good for organized medicine is good for the country.

I further observed:

"Any governmental regulatory body is presumed to be wholly free of influence by special interest groups and hence impartial in its decisions and rulemaking. Yet there is abundant evidence, recent as well as historic, pointing to a tacit agreement between FDA and AMA, whereby each serves the other's interests in a reciprocal way. Each boasts of the other's 'coöperation'."

At the time of Dr. Smith's letter to FDA's medical director, Hubbard's book had been in print only a month and the federal agency had not yet heard of it. Replying to Dr. Smith, the FDA official wrote that "We don't seem to have any information on L. Ron Hubbard or Joseph A. Winter or 'Dianetics'. Further we do not find such names in the local directory."

With AMA's co-operation and continuing insistence, however, this state of innocence on the part of Establishment functionaries did not persist for long.

Meanwhile, AMA's own cloak-and-dagger department was not idle. In keeping with long-standing policy, that organization's Bureau of Investigation remained in the background, but became – and has remained to this day – a prime mover and co-ordinator of the campaign against Dianetics and later, Scientology. The means and methods to those used during World War II and the Cold War that followed, by groups conducting operations which came to be known as psychological warfare.

The basic aim of *sykewar* was to mislead, confuse and incapacitate not only the enemy's armed forces, but the general population as well. The chief weapon was propaganda, disseminated in various guises – news stories, rumours, slanted broadcasts, official statements and false reports of immorality or anti-social behaviour among the opponents' leaders.

The raw data out of which these canards are concocted reach the concealed operators from volunteer informants, paid spies, friends in government offices, and in the case of AMA; from physician members who obtained their information from patients whose close relatives or friends had become interested in Scientology.

AMA's psychological warriors did not use the material they were collecting to launch a straightforward frontal attack on Scientology and its founder. Instead, they employed a practice which the Spanish call *mano ajeno* – that is, using another's hand. Information designed to discredit Scientology and its adherents and to ridicule their beliefs as being the product of an unsound mind, was "planted" with all the media and given to the subsidized hacks who grind out the articles which appear in publications directly controlled by organized medicine. Reprints of these often scurrilous and always hostile accounts were then quoted extensively and given the widest possible circulation.

To give the reader some idea of the magnitude of this operation catspaw, it will suffice to cite but one example. In a single letter to the editor of *Southern California Clergyman*, AMA's Bureau of Investigation enclosed reprints of articles unfavourable to Scientology which had appeared in the following publications: *Today's Health*, *Time*, *Medical News*, *Life*, *Washington Post*, *London Sunday Times*, *Saturday Evening Post*, *Look*, *New York Times* and *Wall Street Journal*.

AMA had previously "co-operated" in providing background material for most if not all of the articles just cited. Thus the medical monopolists could effect a large-scale dissemination of their propaganda without taking any responsibility for it.

To start the ball rolling, and to set the general tone of the knock-out offensive against Scientology, a few months after publication of *Dianetics: The Modern Science of Mental*

Health, Dr. Morris Fishbein wrote a derisive editorial for *Postgraduate Medicine,* in which he disparaged Hubbard, implied that Dr. Winter (who had written an introduction for the book) was a quack; and suggested action by official enforcement agencies against the Dianetic movement.

"The writer of this weird volume suffers apparently from a *cacoethes scribendi,*" he sneered. "Some of his paragraphs are lush outpourings of exuberant diction funnier than anything attempted in the verbal caricatures that distinguished Robert Benchley."

For Dr. Fishbein thus to criticize Hubbard's writing style is but indication of his overweening arrogance. Hubbard is a highly successful professional writer, who for years earned a good livelihood writing books and magazine pieces that had to win their acceptance in a fiercely competitive market-place.

On the other hand, Dr. Fishbein's published prose (written almost exclusively for a captive audience) has never indicated that he possessed any genuine literary talent.

Referring to his fellow AMA member, Dr. J. A. Winter, who had dared to dissent from the medical syndicalist philosophy, Dr. Fishbein wrote:

"Dr. J. A. Winter will no doubt open an office for treatment by the 'dianetic' scheme in Chicago. Los Angeles would be better, but perhaps that gold-mine has already been assigned to some other prospector."

Then Dr. Fishbein hinted at the hard-line strategy AMA intended to adopt in order to destroy Dianetics – use of the police powers vested in governmental regulatory bodies. "Sooner or later," he said, "some official agency will have to give this method [Dianetics] a name – either the practice of medicine, mind-healing, or some other classification covered by the laws of the individual States."

When the foregoing editorial appeared in the September 1950 issue of *Postgraduate Medicine,* Oliver Field, director of AMA's Bureau of Investigation, immediately requested reprints to distribute to a wider audience than that represented in the readership of the professional journal.

There followed a derogatory article by a psychiatrist in the *Journal of the American Medical Association* and later, grossly biased reports in a growing list of lay publications. The great number of large-circulation magazines and newspapers that are literally at the beck and call of the orthodox medical establishment, is in itself a fact that should give pause to any thoughtful person. The editorial staff of almost every American newspaper of any size today will include a medical editor with whom the AMA, as well as other organizations such as Mental Health Federation, American Heart Association, Arthritis and Rheumatism Foundation, American Cancer Society and so on, maintain close ties.

Professional public relations representatives from these groups woo the journalist in various ways, including free lunches and/or drinks at a nearby bar; citations and impressive annual awards for medical journalism; honorary membership in medical societies; and (in the case of the American Cancer Society) expense paid trips around the country to attend symposia at which research teams report on the mythology of progress made in the fight against that disease.

It is hardly surprising, in the light of such an amiable relationship, that when the frequent press releases bearing the familiar insignia of these organizations reach his desk, the medical writer views them with a cordial and uncritical eye. They are, after all, communications from his friends. For him to argue that he faithfully uses the material thus submitted to him only because it is newsworthy and "in the public interest", is a weak and untenable pleading.

To strike any kind of acceptable balance in the news, it would be necessary – no, imperative – at some time or other to report factually on the deficiencies and inhumanity of the medical profession itself – such matters as the careless or excessive use of dangerous new drugs by physicians; the strict businessman approach to the doctor-patient relationship; the "milking" of health insurance policies by both doctors and hospitals with the patient a suffering pawn; or the often villainous practices employed in persecuting reputable and gifted colleagues who refuse to be shackled by the trade-union strictures of the AMA.

These topics, however, are almost never covered by the mass media, and when they must be, as when an important malpractice suit is filed, or a scandal erupts, which even influence in high places cannot conceal, they are played-down or liberally interspersed with extenuating quotes supplied by the accused.

Most of the medical writer's crusading spirit is expended on "quacks" whose sphere of influence affects only an infinitesimal portion of the population; and on health food addicts whose "nutritional nonsense" harms nobody but the allopathic doctors who are deprived of more patients, and the processed food manufacturers, who have fewer customers.

Even if medical writers did not allow personal rapport and pro-establishment bias to colour their treatment of the news, however, it is quite likely that the medical and mental health fields would remain exempt from serious criticism or inquiry into some of their questionable practices. The reason is quite simple: organized medicine also has taken care to make friends in the higher echelons of publishing. Here I speak not from hearsay, but from personal experience.

Some years ago, when I was science editor of a metropolitan daily newspaper in Los Angeles, California (where my responsibility included medical coverage), I once proposed to the managing editor that we undertake an investigative report on a mental health organization whose activities were supported by annual drives for public donations. Some of their practices had appeared to me to be highly irregular, if not unethical.

The managing editor regarded me dourly for a moment, then said: "A member of our publisher's family is on the local executive committee. If you want to start a crusade, why don't you find an outfit that's vulnerable?"

The ties between the newspaper and another local organization – a cancer research foundation, whose administrative costs had earlier attracted my attention – were even closer. In an aggressive circulation drive, the paper announced that a percentage of the money paid for each new subscription would be donated to the medical foundation.

An opposition newspaper wryly suggested a slogan for the campaign: "Watch us grow with cancer."

As AMA's Operation Catspaw continued, Oliver Field, director of the medical fraternity's Bureau of Investigation, compiled an impressive file of published material attacking Dianetics (and later, Scientology) and defaming its founder. From this "black propaganda", he selected those items which apparently he felt would be most damaging to the Scientologists, and these were sent out as enclosures in all his correspondence concerning them. Eventually, he devised a kind of form letter which repeated over and over identical statements to doctors, laymen and casual inquirers alike.

Only in a few instances did Field so far forget his role of psychological warrior as to inject personal statements which, had they become known to Hubbard at the time, would almost certainly have landed the AMA executive in court charged with slander.

For example, in a letter dated June 30, 1952, replying to a query by a lieutenant in the U.S. Marine Corps, Field wrote: "From information in our file, we wonder if Mr. Hubbard is not in need of some psychiatric treatment himself."

Again, in a written communication addressed to a lawyer in Currituck, North Carolina, Field stated: "It is our understanding that Mr. Hubbard, the originator of all this has spent some time in a mental institution."

On at least two occasions, Field told his correspondents

that Scientology was "a scheme to victimize gullible persons".

When newspapers published inaccurate allegations made against Hubbard in a domestic relations court case, Field had the stories photocopied and sent them as additional hand-outs to various correspondents.

The adversary lawyer who had made the derogatory statements available to the press was a Los Angeles attorney known to me and whom I regarded as a publicity seeker who liked to try his cases in the newspaper. My colleagues were also aware of this fact, but that did not deter them from quoting at length the lawyer's hearsay statements and accusations against Hubbard. A wire-service picked up the story and distributed it throughout the country.

The only effective restraint imposed upon journalistic enterprise in the service of the medical trade unionists are the laws of libel. In most cases, the prohibitive cost of legal action places this form of redress beyond the reach of the individual or organization whose reputation is being demolished. But where Scientology is concerned, much to the indignation of both publishers and propagandists, there has been no reluctance to hail the offenders into court.

"We have developed a technique," Bob Thomas told me, "which is notification. We say to somebody who's about to print something: 'You are hereby informed that what you are saying is not true and you should research it to find out if it is true.'

"If they publish it after having disregarded our notification, then there is some chance of getting them on intent. But, of course, proving malicious intent is a can of worms, really. It's pretty easy for them to go in to a judge and say, 'Listen, Your Honour, these people are a bunch of quacks. We just told the truth about them and that's the way it is.' And the judge listens to this and accepts it as evidence. So much depends on whether there is judicial bias."

The effectiveness of Scientology's legal strategy soon became evident in the reduced number of denigrating and at times near-libellous treatments of Hubbard and his followers by the press.

A typical case is that of *The Arizona Republic*, one of the two daily newspapers in Phoenix, Arizona (circulation: 169,536). The medical editor of the paper, a former medical student, had been a member of the Maricopa County Board of Health; honorary member of the County Medical Society; member of the Arizona Society of Medical Technologists; the Arizona Medical Education Foundation; and honorary member of the International Academy of Proctology. Additionally, he was a member of the Board of directors of the Maricopa County Mental Health Association. In 1965, he was recipient of the AMA Medical Journalism Award.

It is not surprising that a close liaison existed between the paper and organized medicine.

In a letter dated May 24, 1969, to Oliver Field at AMA national headquarters, Fred Mitten, executive secretary of the Maricopa County Medical Society (which includes Phoenix) wrote that "some pig – er took our Scientology file. Would you be kind enough to send us a duplicate which would include the British newspaper clippings I have been sending you? *We have a feature writer on the Republic ready to go with a big exposé.*" (Emphasis added.)

Of course, AMA's propaganda department was happy to oblige, and staff associate William J. Monaghan sent a packet of derogatory material reproduced from various publications, both British and American.

However, the projected attack on Scientology ran into an unexpected obstacle. Apparently the exposé had been undertaken without the knowledge or authorization of the paper's executive office. When it came to the attention of the managing editor, he "killed" the series because, he said, he did not want the paper to have to defend itself in a legal action brought against it by the litigation-prone Scientologists.

As Scientology continued to come under attack from

various sources, Hubbard expanded his strike-back strategy to meet the threat.

"We had to establish a separate arm of the church, called the Guardian's Office," Bob Thomas told me, "which deals primarily with defence of the church against attacks of its enemies, who use the media, government agencies. We have had to become experts in such subjects as public relations, the evaluation of data, and all those things germane to a war of ideas.

"The Guardian is, in effect, an executive. He has his own command lines into the organization. Organization executives are trained to filter out any kind of information which deals with certain categories of attack on the environment and to route it to the Guardian's office and it is dealt with there. In this way, the organization can continue functioning quite independently of any source of attack. So, they are free to promote Scientology and to serve the public. Otherwise, they would be very confused by the impact of this constant pressure.

"We have a standard operation procedure (SOP) which provides that any *entheta* reports or attacks be turned over to the bureaux which are concerned. Then there will be co-ordination among legal, and public relations departments, each of which has its own job. In this way, a co-ordinated programme is instituted immediately upon receipt of information concerning an attack."

Over the years, Hubbard had learned from painful experience that it was futile to try to reason with his enemies or to explain the methods and meaning of Scientology to them. They were motivated by implacable hatred of Scientology's philosophy and aims, which were inimical to their private interests. Similarly, co-operation with official or quasi-official groups set up to investigate Scientology availed nothing. The only effective way to meet such a challenge was to counter-attack the moment there was any hostile movement on the part of the adversary.

"*Don't ever* tamely submit to any investigation of us,"

Hubbard told his organizations in a policy letter dated February 15, 1966. "Make it rough, rough on attackers all the way.

"You can get 'reasonable about it' and lose. Sure, we break no laws. Sure, we have nothing to hide. *But* attackers are simply an anti-Scientology *propaganda* agency so far as we are concerned. They have proven they want no facts and will only lie no matter what they discover. So *banish* all ideas that any fair hearing is intended and start our attack with their first breath. Never wait. Never talk about us – only them. Use *their* blood, sex, crime to get headlines. Don't use us.

"I speak from fifteen years of experience in this. There has never been an attacker who was not reeking with crime. All we had to do was look for it and murder would come out.

"They fear our Meter. They fear freedom. They fear the way we are growing. Why?

"Because they have too much to hide.

"When you use *that* rationale, you win. When you go dish-water and say, 'We honest chickens just plain love to have you in the coop, Brer Fox,' we get clobbered. The right response is 'We militant public defenders of the freedom of the people want that there Fox investigated for eating living chickens!' Shift the spotlight to them. No matter how. Do it!"

He added:

"I can count several heavy attacks which folded up by our noisily beginning an investigation of the attacker."

As Scientology organizations proceeded to compile and analyse information concerning the nature and probable source of attacks made on them throughout the world, it became apparent that the assaults emanated from a given point of focus. In a brief submitted to the Commission of Enquiry in South Africa, the Scientologists wrote:

"Finding itself wantonly attacked by governments and by the press, the Church has sought to find whether these attacks were genuine expressions of critical, though uninformed, opinion, or whether they were being instigated and if so, by whom. Without exception they have been found to have been instigated by psychiatrists or psychologists. The Church has further inquired whether these attacks represented spontaneous expressions of opinion by the persons concerned, or whether they were the result of a policy consciously pursued by one or more organizations or groups or people. In almost every case the persons concerned have been members of or connected to a single organization – The World Federation for Mental Health."

The Scientologists having thus identified organized psychiatry as their principal enemy, this is a convenient point at which to examine the background, practices and personnel of political psychiatry; and to define the character and goals of the international Mental Health Movement.

5. *The Crafty Art of Psychopolitics*

Dr. Thomas S. Szasz, a prominent American psychiatrist and outspoken critic of his own discipline as it is presently practised, once described the mental health movement as "essentially Communist ideology in medicine".

The principal features of the movement, he said, are: first, that the individual is regarded as object, rather than subject; second, that the individual is considered unimportant, whereas the group – whether it be the community, society, nation, or mankind as a whole – is considered supremely important; and third, that, in imitation of the physical sciences, the aim of social science (and psychiatry) is the prediction and control of human behaviour. Inherent in this approach is a contempt for man as an autonomous individual: we thus witness the aspiration by a "scientific" elite to control the masses of mankind, whom they consider their inferiors.[1] (p. 219)

The important thing to remember here is that these are not the words of a layman who happens to dislike "head-shrinkers" and all their work, but the considered judgment of a certified psychiatrist who holds a full professorship in his specialty at the State University of New York. In short, he speaks with authority and from first-hand experience.

In his numerous articles, books and lectures, Dr. Szasz has argued – and I believe, convincingly – that the main thrust of contemporary psychiatry is not towards improved measures of prevention and treatment of mental illness, but "toward the creation of a collectivist society, with all this implies for economic policy, personal liberty, and social conformity".[1] (p. 30) Far from reducing the number of cases of mental illness, promoters of the mental health movement *create* more and more cases by extending medical diagnosis to cover everything from petty larceny to political beliefs.

"There is no behaviour or person that a modern psychiatrist cannot plausibly diagnose as abnormal or ill."[2] (p. 35)

Dr. Szasz likens these psychiatric case-finders to the witch-prickers of the seventeenth century – a class of men which made its appearance in Europe during the witchcraft mania and who gained their livelihood by going from town to town to examine suspected men and women for certain insensible spots on their bodies that would indicate that they were witches. The prevalence of witches grew with the growing number of witch-finders.

Similarly, mental illness has grown with the number of psychiatric case-finders in the field.

"After the turn of the century," wrote Dr. Szasz, "and especially following each of the two world wars, the pace of this psychiatric conquest increased rapidly. The result is that, today, particularly in the affluent West, all the difficulties and problems of living are considered psychiatric diseases, and everyone (but the diagnosticians) is considered mentally ill. Indeed, it is no exaggeration to say that life itself is now viewed as an illness that begins with conception and ends with death, requiring, at every step along the way, the skillful assistance of physicians and, especially, mental health professionals."[1] (p. 4)

In a surprisingly candid article appearing in *Psychology Today*, Dr. Anthony M. Graziano, a clinical psychologist of Buffalo, N.Y., stated the case even more succinctly in these words: "In the mental-health industry, illness is our most important product."

Dr. Graziano correctly suggested to his colleagues that they are convincing ever-greater numbers of persons that even minor anxieties which everyone experiences might be symptoms of deeper and more severe problems. "The [mental-health] industry's idealistic campaign rhetoric of public service assures it an annual slice of government and private budgets and a growing catalogue of treatable symptoms that attract an ever-expanding clientele. But this same rhetoric obscures from public view the fact that the treatment available to mental patients is of questionable effectiveness *and may sometimes be destructive.*" (Emphasis added.)[3] (p. 13)

Dr. Graziano apparently assumed that the only reason promoters of mental hygiene indiscriminately label various forms of human behaviour "mental illness", is the lure of government money and private largesse.

There is, however, a far more important motivation behind the whole mental-health movement throughout the world. The statements and activities of the psychopathologists themselves will make that fact clear.

Historically, the master plan for a psychiatric take-over of progressively larger sectors of both social and political life in all countries was first formulated in 1948 at the International Congress on Mental Health, meeting in London.

Attending were delegates from forty-three countries, as well as representatives from the United Nations and the World Health Organization.

Dr. George S. Stevenson, one of the movement's founding members, said of the initial assembly: "A small group of people representing a number of countries and several professions gathered in London to make a covenant to advance mental health on a world basis. Their decision to form the World Federation for Mental Health was a distinct advance over the earlier International Committee for Mental Hygiene in that it saw its job as continuous rather than one of sponsoring congresses periodically."[4]

It was decided that the work of the World Federation would be carried out by affiliated national mental health associations in as many countries as could be brought within its organizational framework. (At this writing 165 member associations in sixty-three countries throughout the world are affiliated with the WFMH.)

In addition to these various national bodies, the WFMH formed important links with the United Nations and its specialized agencies, as well as with the World Health Organization.

Although spokesmen for the UN have recently denied that close ties exist between that organization and the WFMH, one of the Federation's own publications states otherwise:

"The Federation was brought into being partly at the suggestion of UNESCO and the World Health Organization, and was given an official relationship as a consultative body by them in the first few months of its existence. Soon after that we were placed on the register of the Secretary General of the United Nations, which involves a similar relationship to the Economic and Social Council. Later we came on the list of consultative bodies to UNICEF, and on the special list of the International Labour Organization."[5] (p. 12)

The function of the WFMH in relation to these UN agencies, according to Dr. George S. Stevenson, was "to advise, support and prod where needed, just as do the counterpart national and regional mental health bodies in a country or its parts".[4]

With the World Health Organization, the liaison is even more intimate:

"The World Health Organization has in some ways a

closer relationship to us, since its Mental Health Section, whose original program the Federation was asked to outline when it was set up, is the only other international body in this field."[5] (p. 14)

To fully understand the true objectives of the World Federation for Mental Health, it is necessary to examine the beliefs and avowed political aims of the men who worked so long and hard to bring the global organization into being and who have charted its course. Over the years since WFMH was organized, the same names have appeared regularly on one or other of the Federation's boards, councils and roster of officers.

It is generally acknowledged that it was Dr. Brock Chisholm who was the chief architect and prime mover of WFMH. However, most if not all of his associates were known to share his ideas and general views concerning psychiatry's role in the contemporary world.

Dr. Chisholm has defined that role in these words:

"The re-interpretation and eventually eradication of the concept of right and wrong which has been the basis of child training, the substitution of intelligent and rational thinking for faith in the certainties of the old people, these are the belated objectives of practically all effective psychotherapy."[6] (p. 9)

In addition to wiping out the moral concepts of right and wrong and the religious faith of past generations, Dr. Chisholm believed, in common with the radical left, that there should be an economic levelling of society:

"There must be an opportunity to live reasonably for all the people in the world on economic levels which do not vary too widely either geographically or by groups within a population. This is a simple matter of redistribution of material wealth."[7]

According to Dr. Chisholm, and those associated with him in drafting the WFMH Charter, only psychiatrists could achieve these goals.

"Psychiatry," he said, "must now decide what is to be

the immediate future of the human race; no one else can. And this is the prime responsibility of psychiatry."[7]

It was a tall order, but not too tall for the mental-health professionals, who speak of their messianic mission as the remaking of man (or the remoulding of society) if possible, in a single generation.

"Certainly the psychiatrists are not in the least backward in staking out their claim to possessing superior intelligence and know-how with which to alter materially and permanently human behaviour."[6] (p. 6)

This theme – that the whole world is the psychiatrist's experimental laboratory – was repeated not long ago by Dr. Howard P. Rome, senior consultant in psychiatry at the Mayo Clinic, and former president of the American Psychiatric Association. He said:

"Actually, no less than the entire world is a proper catchment area for present-day psychiatry, and psychiatry need not be appalled by the magnitude of the task."[8] (p. 727)

Quite in keeping with this ambitious plan for global domination is one of the principal goals of WFMH: world citizenship. An editorial appearing in the Federation's 1968 *Bulletin* cites it as the *first* aim in the minds of the founders when they established WFMH in 1948.

"Outmoded loyalties" are due to "the lag in citizen maturity." Part of the programme of the Federation is aimed at re-educating the public away from such political naiveté.

In a book distributed by the National Association for Mental Health (in the U.S.) it is stated:

"Principles of mental health cannot be successfully furthered in any society unless there is a progressive acceptance of the concept of world citizenship."[9]

What are the implications of labelling a citizen immature because he believes in loyalty to his own country as a primary allegiance, to take precedence over supra-national loyalty? In the practice of psychiatry today it is very often a step towards declaring the same individual mentally ill. It lays the groundwork for *political control.*

A citizen who feels that his first allegiance is due to his own country will resist the efforts of those groups he considers to be subversive or inimical to his political heritage. But a psychiatrist may interpret any suspicion of hidden enemies in our society and government as paranoia. Dr. George S. Stevenson has already hinted at this diagnosis. He described as mentally ill any person who is "suspicious of others and sees an enemy, *perhaps a Communist* lurking behind every acquaintance".[10] (Italics mine.)

Similarly, scepticism or dissent regarding such matters as extension of long-term loans to Russia; compulsory sex-education in the schools; or liberal re-interpretation of obscenity laws – all may be regarded by the psychopathologists as symptoms of "basic insecurity".

As we shall see later, the use of psychiatry to silence dissent and to evade due process of law in the United States is already a *fait accompli.* As Dr. Szasz has observed, the psychiatrist is the only person in the U.S. who is empowered by law to deprive people of their freedom when they have not been convicted of any crime. This is also true of other countries where involuntary commitment without a court hearing is legal.

Given the broad definition of mental illness already cited by leading psychiatrists, this is a chilling fact that should be carefully weighed by every citizen who lives in those countries.

Public uneasiness about psychiatry does, in fact, already exist. There is a general consensus the world over that psychiatrists are an odd-ball lot. No other discipline in medicine has been so rich a source of bar-room jokes or has provided so many themes for cartoons and satires.

The attitude of the average man has been and continues to be that where crazy people are concerned, it takes one to treat one.

In the vulgate, psychiatrists are known by such epithets

as sickyatrist, head shrinker, brain bender, dingaling doctor and psycho.

Such expressions clearly show that the majority of people hold the profession in very low esteem, a fact further attested to by actual statistics. A recent survey revealed that only 16 per cent of persons who have emotional difficulties consult a psychiatrist. Of that number, a great many do so only at the urging of relatives, friends or marriage partners.

The behaviour of the psychiatrists themselves, both public and private, has done much to reinforce this widely-held notion that they are mortals of a different and more exotic clay. Accounts of their hare-brain proposals or shocking escapades are a recurring constant in the daily newspaper and on television. One or two typical examples will serve to indicate the type of lunacies for which they are noted. (There are available even more outré instances than those which follow, but I forbear citing them because they would only provoke the total incredulity of the reader.)

A British psychiatrist recently accomplished a feat that most persons would pronounce impossible: he shocked a Swedish audience with his "liberal" ideas on sex and social behaviour.

Addressing a gathering of 300 young people in Stockholm, he advised them to copulate in the corridors and to finance a youth revolution by stealing from supermarkets.

To set the theme for his talk, the psychiatrist, dressed in a black fur maxi-coat, ardently kissed a girl, then walked to the microphone and to the tune of *Glory, Glory Hallelujah* sang: "Glory, glory, psychotherapy; Glory, glory, sexuality . . ."

One member of the astonished audience said afterwards: "I was probably quite wrong, but I thought he was drunk, under the influence of drugs or something, or perhaps mad."

It is important to note here that the speaker was formerly in charge of the mental health department of a large London hospital.

In the United States, one of the British doctor's colleagues not long ago added to the doubts and suspicions that generally hang over their profession when he suggested that psychiatric chemicals might be added to community reservoirs to control human behaviour. "Then everyone will relax."

Or again:

Writing in a professional journal, an American psychiatrist of ripe experience told how he had treated tensed-up wives by kissing, undressing, genital manipulation and sexual intercourse. Such unorthodox therapy was necessary, he explained, in order to act out what he termed "overt transference".

Husbands who had to foot the bill were thus paying $25 an hour to be cuckolded.

Striking a familiar pose of his profession, that of the dedicated healer who is ready to undergo personal hardship or at least discomfort in order to restore his patient to perfect health, the practitioner asserted that: "The demands which this technique makes on the analyst are as grave as any difficulty encountered in the practice of medicine."

The problem was particularly acute in the case of the unattractive patient. "Then it's tough, as tough as a surgical operation."

This psychoanalyst made it clear that he was not singular in his transformation of the traditional couch into an altar of Venus. He said many psychiatrists had told him they too employed the same methods and regarded them as a legitimate mode of treatment.

Another American psychiatrist confirmed the statement. He declared: "It's widespread from coast to coast; and it produces results."

In my own experience, I once knew a Beverly Hills, California, secretary who went to her psychiatrist for an afternoon romp in the nude as faithfully as she went to her hairdresser. Sometimes, she reported, other patients joined in for a group therapy session, which included a variety of Paphian fun and games.

It is hardly necessary to point out that all psychiatrists do not indulge in practices of the kind just described. But a surprising number do. And the fact that they are tolerated by their colleagues and, in many cases, hold important posts in professional societies, would seem to indicate that they are not as offensive to other members of their discipline as they are to the lay public. It is fair to say that silence gives assent.

Even more important, so long as they are qualified to practice, they hold an awesome power of life and death over patients, many of whom are treated involuntarily with a variety of terrifying psychiatric interventions, including lobotomy, convulsive shock therapy, powerful drugs and so on.

To entrust such men with the treatment – indeed, with the lives – of individuals described as mentally ill, is in itself a flagrant violation of the most basic human rights.

L. Ron Hubbard first came into open conflict with organized psychiatry soon after publication of *Dianetics: The Modern Science of Mental Health.*

As indicated earlier, Hubbard rejected what he termed brutal assaults on the brain (radical surgery, electric convulsive shock and lobotomy) which form a routine part of psychiatric practice. He also boldly asserted that Dianetics was a better system of therapy than any known to orthodox psychiatry.

Not only that, but some of the political manoeuvrings of prominent mental-health professionals had begun to claim his close attention.

At that time, leaders of the mental health movement were preparing prototype legislation they hoped to push through the U.S. Congress, which would radically alter involuntary commitment procedures.

From its earliest conception, the mental hygiene movement had included among its prime objectives the involvement of government in its programmes. Such involvement would make it easier for the psychiatric groups to obtain grants-in-aid as well as to secure passage of enabling legislation.

In this aim the proponents of what Dr. Szasz has called a Therapeutic State have been highly successful.

In 1946, the U.S. Congress passed a National Mental Health Act, which set up the National Institute of Mental Health as a psychiatric research and training centre and provided grants-in-aid for the development of community clinics throughout the country.

The bill also authorized funds to be made available to both public and private agencies for psychiatric research, training psychiatrists and psychiatric social workers, clinical psychologists and psychiatric nurses. It included financial assistance to states in developing community health programmes and consultations.

Mental health was on its way towards becoming a major industry.

Once these centres were established and functioning, an advertising campaign, operating under the guise of a mental health education programme, was launched to attract clients. Dr. Szasz describes the activity thus:

"Mental health education is an effort to lure unsuspecting persons into becoming clients of the community mental health services. Then, having created a demand – or, in this case, perhaps merely the appearance of one – the industry expands: this takes the form of steadily increasing expenditures for existing mental hospitals and clinics for creating new, more highly automated factories called 'community mental health centres'."[1] (p. 41)

On the state level, the problem of mental health occupied an increasingly important place on the agenda of the Annual Governors Conference each year after its first introduction in 1949. Representatives of the psychiatric fraternity cited statistical evidence which purported to prove that mental illness is the nation's number one health problem; that every other bed in the country's hospitals was a "mental bed"; that perhaps one in every nine persons could look forward to a mental breakdown at some time or other during their lifetimes (a self-fulfilling prophecy, considering the ever-wider classification of problems in living as "mental illness" by the profession).

These figures were quoted with the same air of certainty than an epidemiologist might asume in predicting the probable incidence of a communicable disease such as gonorrhoea. Yet mental illness is not a disease entity. If it were, as Dr. Szasz has observed, one could *catch* mental illness as one catches a cold. One could *have* or *harbour* it; one might transmit it to others; and finally, by employing the proper treatment, it could be cured.

The truth is that there are no precise clinical criteria for determining mental illness as a true illness or disease. Definitions differ among authorities in the field, depending upon the individual psychiatrist's personal orientation. To mental health professionals of a political stripe, patriotism is considered a form of mental illness that should be treated by psychiatric intervention.

The same is true of religion. A deep religious faith is regarded as a form of psychoneurosis if not psychosis, by the majority of psychiatrists practicing today.

Aside from a handful of Catholic and even fewer devout Protestant practitioners, there is virtually universal agreement in the profession that religion has an adverse effect on mental health.

This implacable hostility to spirituality has prompted many attacks on the personality of Jesus Christ, whom leading psychopathologists have pronounced insane. Typical of these "diagnoses" is the statement of an American psychiatrist that, "Everything that we know about him [Christ] conforms so perfectly to the clinical picture of paranoia that it is hardly conceivable that people can even question the diagnosis."[11]

With the exception of an early work by Dr. Albert Schweitzer, *The Psychiatric Study of Jesus*, published in

1913, I know of no major work by a psychiatrist which seeks to challenge or to repudiate this view.

It should occasion no surprise that psychiatrists would thus undertake to diagnose the mental condition of a man who lived almost 2,000 years ago and about whom no *clinical* details exist. For, while claiming that mental illness is a disease (which can be determined only by personal examination and/or laboratory tests), psychiatrists do not hesitate to declare persons psychotic whom they have never seen.

When Senator Barry Goldwater became a candidate for President of the United States, no fewer than 1,189 members of the American Psychiatric Association (who were opposed to his political views) declared him to be "psychologically unfit to serve as President". Many of them asserted that he was suffering from paranoid schizophrenia, and that he was "a potentially dangerous man".

Senator Goldwater's running mate, William E. Millar, was diagnosed as "a man as hostile and semi-paranoid as [Goldwater] himself".

On the eve of the 1972 national elections, when President Nixon was seeking his second term in office, a "psycho-historical inquiry" into the President's personality was published. Bruce Mazlish, who wrote the book had never interviewed Mr. Nixon, but this did not discourage him in psychoanalysing the Chief Executive.

An example of what can happen when a career politician does consult a psychiatrist concerning simple problems in living is provided by the case of Senator Thomas Eagleton of Missouri, Democratic nominee for U.S. vice-president in 1972. Senator Eagleton's medical history became a national issue and was said to be partly responsible for his party's loss of the election.

Soon after Eagleton's nomination, the press revealed that he had previously undergone electric shock treatments for what he described as nervous exhaustion. The public, which rightly regards that kind of psychiatric intervention with great apprehension, reacted unfavourably to the news and the Senator's party asked him to withdraw.

Eagleton thus had good reason to regret his having placed himself in the hands of the mental health professionals. But certainly, he was not the first public figure to become so involved. Psychiatrists have treated presidents, legislators and judges. Indeed, Dr. F. Cloutier, former president of the World Federation of Mental Health, once suggested that top office-holders be assisted at all times by a psychiatrist-adviser.

As early as 1938, H. D. Lasswell, writing in the professional journal, *Psychiatry*, proposed that psychiatrists "cultivate closer contact with the rulers of society, in the hope of finding the means of inducing them to overcome the symbolic limitations which prevent them from utilizing their influence for the prompt re-arrangement of insecurity producing routines". (Translation: Psychiatrists should gain control over the world's leaders and use them to restructure society along the lines suggested by Dr. Chisholm and his school.)

The boldest move by proponents of the mental health programme to extend their control over an entire population was the Alaska Mental Health Act, introduced in the U.S. Congress in 1955.

As an unabashed circumvention of the American Bill of Rights, this measure was without precedent in the legislative history of that country. Under its terms, anyone at any time is subject to seizure and involuntary commitment to a mental institution without recourse to due process guaranteed by the Fifth Amendment to the U.S. Constitution.

A prominent Los Angeles jurist, Superior Court Judge Joseph M. Call, who made a careful study of the act from the legal stand-point, characterized it as "totalitarian government at its best".

"Under this section [104(b)], any health, welfare or

police officer who has reason to believe that an individual is mentally ill and therefore likely to injure himself or others if not immediately restrained pending examination and certification by a licensed physician, may take the individual into physical custody and transport him to a mental asylum. This section, in effect, practically nullifies every constitutional safeguard to be found in the Federal Constitution for the protection of the individual. It is the police state working at its best.

1. It permits no examination of any type.
2. No statement of probable cause need be filed under oath to support the issuance of a warrant of arrest or apprehension.
3. No judge or magistrate need issue a warrant of arrest.
4. No examination is permitted of the patient by the patient's own physician.
5. No examination is provided for by any physician.
6. No trial is permitted by a judge.
7. No trial is permitted by a jury.

"This section under these conditions permits the patient to be held in custody and without bail up to a period of 5 days under rules and regulations to be prescribed by the head of the hospital. By the end of 5 days the head of the hospital is authorized to designate an examiner to make an examination, and upon the certification of the examiner that in his opinion the patient (1) is mentally ill or (2) is likely to injure himself or others if allowed at liberty, he is forthwith committed to further confinement and custody under this certificate.

"Let us lay this section of the Health Act side by side with Article VI of the Bill of Rights of the Federal Constitution and see what we find. We see that under the Constitution in all criminal prosecutions the accused shall enjoy:

1. The right to a speedy and public trial.
2. The right to be informed of the nature of the charge preferred against him.

3. The right to be represented by an attorney at all stages of the proceedings.
4. The right to trial by an impartial jury.
5. The right to be confronted by witnesses against him.
6. The right to subpoena witnesses in his own behalf and for his own defense.

"And when we further square up these provisions of the Health Act against Article VI of the Bill of Rights, we find under the Constitution that the right of people to be secure in their persons against unreasonable seizures (of the person) shall not be violated, and no warrant of apprehension shall be issued but upon probable cause, under oath and particularly describing the person or persons to be seized.

"Section V of our Bill of Rights states that no person shall be deprived of life, liberty, or property without due process of law. There can clearly be no denial of the fact that Sections 103 and 104 of the Mental Health Act deny the individual his liberty in advance of commitment to an insane asylum and deny him any of the safeguards specified in Articles IV and VI of the Bill of Rights and, as such, constitute a clear-cut denial of due process of law.

"And at this point it should be clearly pointed out and stressed that all of the foregoing proceedings could be accomplished without the patient's knowledge or that his mental condition was being questioned in any respect whatsoever. And at the time of commitment – for want of any subsequent affirmative action – however induced – the patient could be confined in the mental institution for the rest of his natural life."[12] (pp. 41–3)

An important feature of the bill was its broad, ambiguous definition of mental illness: "The term 'mentally ill individual' means an individual having a psychiatric *or other disease* which substantially impaires his mental health or an individual who is mentally defective or *mentally retarded*." (Emphasis added.)

Who, then, would decide whether an individual is mentally ill? According to the Act, any "interested party or parties", which it defines as "the legal guardian, spouse, parent or parents, adult children, other close adult relatives, or an interested, responsible adult friend of a mentally ill individual or a patient".

Dr. Lewis Albert Alesen, an eminent California physician and formerly Chief of Staff of the giant Los Angeles County General Hospital, who was deeply disturbed by these commitment procedures, spelled out the meaning of the Act in these words:

"An individual, a so-called proposed patient, could be seized by a police or other peace officer in his home or in the street, and transported against his will to a mental hospital where he could be forcibly examined and subjected to any type of therapy thought best, including drugs and narcotics, and the various practices of modern psychiatry including hypnotism, conditioned reflex therapy, shock therapy, and yes, even lobotomy if the doctors in charge thought such techniques indicated, even before the individual had been legally heard and his true mental status actually established by what we Americans have been trained from birth to regard as justifiable legal procedures. During this preliminary period of hospitalization authorized by the bill as an emergency procedure on medical certification, the patient might well be held without opportunity to contact family, friends, or legal counsel for a period not greater than fifteen days, but during such preliminary period ample time would have been given for all manner of brain washing and brain changing. This may seem fantastic, and it may be contended that no real physician conscientiously practicing under the requirements of his Hippocratic oath would resort to such tactics, but nonetheless the provisions are there, and the poor proposed patient has no legal protection against the conscienceless experimenter or the tool of a political regime which deliberately designs to silence all opposition by this expedient.

"Without the protection of the Fifth Amendement and the due process of law it guarantees, the way is wide open for involuntary commitment to mental institutions on the basis of political reprisal, avarice, and cupidity of relatives, and the malice and jealousy of neighbours or enemies."[12] (pp. 37, 39)

As Dr. Alesen pointed out, the Alaska bill followed almost exactly the provisions of earlier prototype legislation known as *A Draft Act Governing Hospitalization of the Mentally Ill*, put together by Dr. George Stevenson, medical director of the National Association for Mental Health and a founding member of WFMH, together with other promoters of the movement.

The Draft Act was a skeleton bill intended for use by federal and all state legislatures in adopting a uniform law covering involuntary commitment procedures. It is significant that the well-settled legal definition of psychopathology – *insane* – does not appear anywhere in the Draft Act, nor in the Alaska Mental Health Act based on it.

One of the first to denounce the Alaska bill and to mobilize civic groups in formidable opposition to its passage was L. Ron Hubbard. And if his thunderous invective at times seemed to have an obsessional tinge, it was only because he had learned that the American public no longer listens to anything moderately stated.

Hubbard called the measure the Siberia Bill because, he said, under its provisions any man, woman, or child could be seized and transferred without trial to an Alaskan Siberia being set up under authorization of the Act. There, the allegedly mentally ill person, deprived of all human and civil rights, could be detained forever. A cleverly legalized way of railroading political enemies, personal opponents and other "undesirables" into permanent oblivion à la USSR.

Proponents of the legislation asserted that Hubbard was deliberately misreading the section of the Act covering transfer of non-resident patients to the (then) Territory of Alaska.

Hubbard and his followers answered that the Act was foot-in-the door legislation that clearly provided for Alaska to make reciprocal agreements with any or all of the States for a wholesale transfer of patients. In fact, prototype legislation had already been drafted, and was embodied in the Connecticut Health Compact that unequivocally authorized such an involuntary transfer of patients.

The legislative manoeuvring which preceded final passage of the bill clearly supported Hubbard's charges.

To save the measure from outright defeat in the face of the formidable and growing opposition to it, the Act's proponents agreed to an amendment proposed by Senator Barry Goldwater, one provision of which would specifically prohibit the transfer of patients from anywhere in the U.S. to insane asylums in Alaska. The Senate sub-committee to whom the bill had been referred, deleted this restriction.

Likewise cut out of the Act was a section of the Goldwater amendment guaranteeing humane treatment of individuals seized as being mentally ill; and another reaffirming the patient's right to a writ of *habeas corpus*.

On the House side, Constitutional protection of the individual fared no better. A provision in the original bill had made it a crime to willfully cause, conspire with or assist another to cause the unwarranted hospitalization of anyone under terms of the Act. However, at the instigation of some unnamed member of the House Committee on Interior and Insular Affairs, this safeguard was also removed.

How could the law-makers satisfactorily explain these indefensible deletions? The only conclusion that issues from such ruthless contempt for due process was that Hubbard and other critics of the bill were right: the secret aim of the legislation was social control.

Even the manner in which the measure was rammed through the Congress suggests the heavy-handed strategy of private interests rather than the carefully considered procedure of responsible law-makers. According to Dr.

Lewis A. Alesen, cited above, the bill was passed by a voice vote in the House, after only two hours of debate. Dr. Alesen correctly observes: "It is reasonable to think that these circumstances indicate the lack of quorum of House members when the measure was adopted."[12] (p. 45)

The measure's passage through the Senate was marked by the same unseemly haste and want of deliberation.

I have treated at length the Alaska Mental Health Act because it was the first major piece of legislation mental health groups were successful in steering through Congress. In design and purpose, it was a prototype of other bills which the same sponsoring organizations have since pushed through both national and state legislatures.

Congress has continued voting funds for expansion of the Community Mental Health Centers programme, initiated in 1963, which provides for setting up "all-purpose mental health" establishments across the nation. Public Law 88–164 scheduled the opening of 500 such centres by 1970.

It cannot be too strongly emphasized that the mental health professionals who plan and direct the activities of these centres are mainly concerned with social issues which they define as mental illness. Dr. Szasz argues that such programmes are really modes of coerced behaviour and control. Let us hear him again:

"They establish themselves as agents of social control and at the same time disguise their punitive interventions in the semantic and social trappings of medical practice."[2] (p. 136)

In the light of these observations, it becomes an ominous fact that in the United States 98 per cent of the care for the so-called mentally ill is provided by federal, state and local governments. In Great Britain, it has been estimated that the proportion is approximately the same. In the Soviet Union, the figure is 100 per cent and all psychiatrists are in the service of the government.

For a clear idea of the dangers that lurk in State

established psychiatry, we have only to look towards Russia, where that system has reached its full maturity.

During the reign of Stalin, political enemies (actual or potential) as well as those suspected of deviation from the officially-proclaimed Communist line, were simply taken out and shot *en masse*, or sent to Siberia to die a slow death in the slave camps. As a dictator whose power was absolute, the Soviet mass-murderer had little use for psychiatrists. He did not pretend that the countless victims seized by his secret police were being incarcerated for their own good, as a therapeutic measure. Like Hitler in his attitude towards the mental defectives, Jews and gypsies of Germany, he just wanted them liquidated.

Following de-Stalinization in the USSR, and the attendant need to establish the appearance of justice in Soviet courts, the Kremlin oligarchy had to find some respectable means of continuing their despotic rule. They urgently required some extra-judicial means of social and political control.

This is precisely the point at which psychiatry gained ascendancy in Russia. Writers with a thirst for liberty, drones and dissenters were no longer brought before legal tribunals where their side of the case could receive at least a token hearing, thereby proving a source of embarrassment to the regime. Instead, they were seized and handed over to psychiatrists as citizens suffering from "mental illness".

A leading Russian forensic psychiatrist, quoted in *Time* magazine, stated the Soviet position unequivocally:

"Why bother with political trials when we have psychiatric clinics?"[13]

Community mental health centres (called dispensaries in the Soviet Union) have been established throughout the USSR, just as they have been set up in the United States. "Russia's social structure has enabled psychiatry to go out into communities and actively search for persons in need of treatment," declared Dr. B. A. Lebedev, prominent Soviet psychiatrist and a medical director of the World Health Organization.[14] (p. 1)

The recent case of Zhores Medvedev, an eminent Russian geneticist, highlights with disturbing clarity how easily mental hospitals may become political prisons in disguise.

Medvedev's troubles began when he published an attack on the scientifically discredited theories of Stalin's favourite scientist, T. D. Lysenko. For that "offence" he was discharged from the position he had held at a radiological institute near Moscow. Then he compounded his crime by writing a study of the State censorship, surveillance and harrassment that restricts intellectual activity in Russia today. The literary underground smuggled the work through the Iron Curtain and published in the West – an unpardonable sin in the eyes of the Communist hierarchy.

Medvedev was seized and sent, without trial, to a Soviet insane asylum. The diagnosis of his case by Russian psychiatrists bears a chilling resemblance to professional opinions voiced by their opposite numbers in the West concerning the mental condition of persons whose political views and social behaviour were unacceptable. Medvedev, said the Soviet psychiatrists, had a "split personality, expressed in the need to combine the scientific work in his field with publicist activities; an overestimation of his own personality; a deterioration in recent years of the quality of his scientific work; an exaggerated attention to detail in his publicist writing; lack of a sense of reality; poor adaption to the social environment".[13]

Before the Western reader indulges himself in the smug and wholly unjustified satisfaction of believing that such a terrible injustice could not occur in "the free world", I hasten to assure him that the truth is quite otherwise.

Consider, for example, the case of the late Ezra Pound, one of the most distinguished figures in the history of American literature. Following World War II, Pound was indicted for treason because of statements he had made in broadcasts from Mussolini's Italy, where he had long resided. Pound declared himself ready to prove his innocence in a court of law; but he was not permitted to do so. Instead, under Section 4244 of the United States Code which (I believe, unconstitutionally) allows a federal judge, *upon motion of the prosecuting U.S. Attorney,* to order an accused person sent without a hearing to a mental institution "to be examined as to his mental condition", by one or more psychiatrists. Pound was handed over to the mental health professionals.

Dr. Winfred Overholser, one of the four psychiatrists who examined Pound, reported to the Court that: "He insists that his broadcasts were not treasonable. He is abnormally grandiose, is expansive and exuberant in manner, exhibiting pressure of speech, discursiveness, and distractability. In our opinion, with advancing years his personality, for many years abnormal, has undergone further distortion to the extent that he is now suffering from a paranoid state."

Dr. Overholser then added: "He is, in other words, insane and mentally unfit for trial, and is in need of care in a mental hospital."[15] (p. 37)

Ezra Pound was committed to the insane asylum and held there for thirteen years. He was released only in response to growing protests against his incarceration. Dr. Overholser continued to oppose the poet's being set free, insisting that Pound was "permanently and incurably insane".

Upon being released from the asylum, Pound returned to Rapallo, Italy, where he spent his last years quietly and quite sanely despite the terrifying experience of having been confined to a madhouse for thirteen years – surely an ordeal to test the temper of the most resilient mind.

But that was not the final cruelty and humiliation to be dealt the old poet at the hands of his implacable enemies, who dominate the academic as well as the political centres of power in his native land. Early in 1972, Pound, then eighty-six, was informed that he would be given an honorary degree from the University of Maine in recognition of his great contribution to American literature. Pound accepted "with great pleasure" and prepared to journey to the U.S. to receive the degree in person.

Then he was informed that the degree was not approved, after all, and could not be awarded. English Professor Carroll Terrell, whose non-political view of literature had led him to propose the degree, was quoted as saying it was all "a ghastly blunder"; opposition to the honour had been too great or, rather, too influential.

Here at its rankest was an illustration of the cynical ambivalence which characterizes intellectual life in America today. Honorary degrees have been impressed upon Marxists, anarchists, Communists and teachers of violent revolution, with the pleading that cultural and educational freedom demand the broadest tolerance of unpopular political viewpoints.

Yet a major poet, none of whose work is concerned with political themes and whom mature European critics class with the greatest of his contemporaries, was denied a small honour because of an alleged offence that occurred more than thirty years previously and for which he had never been tried nor given an opportunity to exonerate himself.

Only a short time after the disgraceful University of Maine affair, the American Academy of Arts and Sciences announced that, for unexplained reasons, it would not award its $2,000 Emerson-Thoreau Medal in 1972. It was later learned that the Academy's literary committee had recommended Ezra Pound for the award, but the governing council had rejected him, again citing his Italian broadcasts during World War II.

That was too much for Biologist Jerome Y. Lettvin of the Massachusetts Institute of Technology, who resigned his membership in protest.

"Had you decided that Pound was an indifferent poet and so deserved no prize," he wrote, "then you would have no need to study his human failings. But you decided he was a good poet. And then you decided not to award him because you disapproved of the man but not his poetry. I will have no part of it."[16] (p. 23)

To return to the Russian system of dealing with social or political undesirables as mentally ill (and it is different from the American system only in extent, not in kind), it has been only recently that organized protests by writers and scientists have put Soviet authorities on the defensive. Yet, almost a decade ago a Russian writer named Valery Tarsis published in England a book called *Ward 7*, relating in detail the story of his confinement in a Moscow psychiatric hospital because his views were regarded as deviationist by the Kremlin.

"To Russian 'scientific psychiatry'," wrote Dr. Szasz, "Valery Tarsis was mentally ill; to American 'scientific psychiatry', Ezra Pound was mentally ill."[1] (p. 111)

It was not Tarsis, but another Soviet writer, Vladamir Bukovsky, who became a *cause celebre* in the long struggle of the Russian intelligensia to direct world attention to the political prisoners immured in KGB-controlled mental wards.

One group of fifty-two Soviet intellectuals, led by a prominent physicist, Andrei Sakharov, laid the case before the United Nations in the vain hope that the international body could or would seek amnesty for Bukovsky.

In an open letter circulated by the Russian underground during his latest detention, Bukovsky's mother wrote: "His only misdemeanour in fact was that he had recounted for the whole world the practice of placing people who think differently in Soviet psychiatric hospitals under the pretext of mental illness."

In the face of growing world concern about the publicized cases in the USSR, several psychiatric organizations, the WFMH among them, issued statements denouncing the practice of misusing psychiatric diagnosis to suppress dissent.

But their belated protests sounded a little hollow when measured against the lavish praise they had earlier accorded Russian institutional psychiatry in their professional journals, lectures and reports.

It was precisely this argument, in fact, that was used by Dr. Andrei Snezhnevsky, chief psychiatrist of the Soviet Ministry of Health, in keeping the topic off the agenda of the World Psychiatric Association conference, held in Mexico City in the autumn of 1971.

Dr. Snezhnevsky pointed out that in 1967 a group of American mental health officials who had toured Russian mental hospitals, found nothing to condemn in the Russian system. According to an article by Dr. Zigmond M. Lebensohn, in the *American Journal of Psychiatry* (November 5, 1968) the "mission team" to which Dr. Snezhevsky referred was composed of "seven seasoned experts . . . a prominent jurist, a public health administrator, a well-known mental-health lobbyist and four highly experienced psychiatrists".

"Prior to Stalin's death in 1953," wrote Dr. Lebensohn, "American psychiatrists had little first-hand knowledge of what was going on in Soviet medicine – even less in Soviet psychiatry. Since 1956, however, psychiatric pilgrims travelling singly or in groups have been wending their way in a steady stream to the main fonts of Soviet psychiatry."

Dr. Lebensohn's choice of the word *pilgrim* – commonly understood to mean a religious devotee who journeys to a shrine – reveals much.

The article stressed the fact that the 1967 tour was not a once-over-lightly visit, but an in-depth study of the Communists' methods: "Their report merits careful study by all Americans interested in broadening their horizons. It is a tribute to the industry and zeal of the members of the mission that they succeeded in overcoming numerous obstacles, administrative and otherwise, to attain their objectives. As a result, they were able to see more and to report in greater depth than any previous group in recent history.

"For the first time *we can get a clear picture of the symbiotic relationship between Soviet psychiatry and Soviet law.* For the first time we can see their efficient system of emergency psychiatric services in action. For the first time we can see clearly how the Soviet organization of mental health services permits their psychiatric manpower (and woman-power) to be efficiently used in hospitals, factories, dispensaries, workshops and schools." (Emphasis added.)

The article then added conclusively: "The experienced members of this important mission have carefully scrutinised many facets of Soviet psychiatry and have emerged with a remarkably favorable estimate of its effectiveness."

As Dr. Lebensohn has informed us, members of the 1967 official Mission on Mental Health were not the only U.S. "pilgrims" to wend their way to Soviet psychiatric "fonts" and come away with only the warmest feelings (even veneration) for the collectivist Pavlovian practice of psychiatry. A considerable number of individual practitioners have also spent much time in the Soviet mental wards, clinics and sheltered workshops where their dedicated colleagues are doing so much to help shape what Russian psychiatrists themselves call their "therapeutic society". All have agreed that, "in the current atmosphere of reassessing mental health programs, it is time to learn from everyone's experience, regardless of ideology or political orientation".

The foregoing statement is contained in a report by Dr. Henry P. David who, during his three-year tenure as associate director of the World Federation for Mental Health, "travelled extensively in Eastern Europe and the Soviet Union".

Dr. David noted (apparently with approval, certainly without disapproval) that "Therapists vigorously engaged in re-education, suggesting values and standards of behaviour they considered realistic, correct and socially desirable. *The ultimate measure of improvement was the patient's behavioural change.*" (Emphasis added.)

This is another way of saying that mental health in Russia is measured by how closely the individual conforms to the politically acceptable behaviour pattern set by the state.

If we are to judge by what its leading spokesmen say and what we read in their literature, that is also one of the principal goals of the mental health crusaders.

Before leaving the subject, there is another aspect of Soviet psychiatry which deserves our attention. It is psychopolitics or the use of trained operatives in the fields of psychiatry and psychology to produce chaos, violence and mutual distrust among the populations of capitalist countries.

The Scientologists have faciliated the widest possible distribution of a booklet dealing with this topic, entitled *Brainwashing: A Synthesis of the Russian Textbook on Psychopolitics.* Owing to the fact that the authorship of the text is somewhat obscure, critics of Scientology have intimated that the whole idea was something Hubbard dreamed up to discredit mental health organizations.

The proof (if proof is needed) that such is not the case lies in the fact that most of the information and comment contained in *Brainwashing* has been stated elsewhere by recognized scholars who had no connection whatever with Scientology.

For example, in *Protracted Conflict*, Strausz-Hupe, Kantner, Dougherty and Cottrell, cited as one of the chief aims of Communist psychological warfare "the creation in the ruling, upper and intellectual classes of non-Communist societies, of frustration, confusion, pessimism, guilt, fear, defeatism, hopelessness and neurosis; of *oblomovism* or *nevolya*, in essence, the psychological destruction of anti-Communist leadership".

It is an ominous fact that the statement of Communist

112 / *The Hidden Story of Scientology*

aims just quoted is also a deadly accurate description of the middle and upper classes in America today.

Just as the idea of a "generation gap", being boldly asserted and plausibly maintained, produced in our society the condition it describes, so the concept of a "sick society" insistently urged upon us by the mental health professionals is producing the psycho-neurotic populace it postulates. One of the most significant changes in public attitude, in fact, has been the uncritical and widespread acceptance of the idea that mental illness in Western countries (especially the U.S.) has reached virtually epidemic proportions and now constitutes a real threat to the survival of a sane, orderly society.

A recent expansion of this concept has been the new psychiatric technique called "crisis intervention", practiced in the Los Angeles County Hospital. This notion is based upon the assumption – asserted as a medical fact – that there is a period in *every* person's life, lasting from four to six weeks when he shows all the symptoms of madness.

During such times any of us might try to assassinate the President, rape the girl next door or engage in other kinds of abnormal behaviour. We must be caught in time and given psychotherapy at once to prevent a long-term mental illness. According to a World Federation for Mental Health bulletin, a team of nurses, social workers, therapists, ministers and psychiatrists are on the lookout for such "crises", and deal with them promptly.

It is safe to predict that this new mental hygiene product will soon be put on the intellectual market alongside such packaged moonshine as "identity crisis".

As we have previously noted, the principal aim of Soviet community-based psychiatry is the modification of individual behaviour to conform to state-established patterns.

"There is a relative de-emphasis of personal needs in favour of the primacy of the collective to which the individual is expected to yield," wrote Dr. Henry P. David in his report on mental health in the Soviet Union.

The same statement fairly describes the main thrust of community mental health programmes in America. Whether they go by such names as operant conditioning or group encounter, they are in fact lineal descendants of the classical Pavlovian technique. Their chief purpose is not therapeutic improvement of psychotic patients, but the political coercion of the non-conforming individuals. Their interventions always result in progressive enslavement to and dependence upon the state. The totalitarian must eradicate at all costs that precious "island of separateness", the independent life and thought of the free man, which allow him to question or to challenge the values of a totalitarian ideology.

In harmony with this Marxist concept of the mentally healthy man as one most fully identified with the collective, leading psychiatrists have redefined individuality as loneliness and alienation, and regard it as "mental illness' requiring treatment.

The same notion has been introduced generally into sociology, literature and religion, with heavy emphasis being placed upon the "need to relate", to "become involved". Criminals and the assassins of public figures are always depicted in the media as "loners", who didn't "fit in", and who acted out of madness, not as part of a far-reaching, international conspiracy.

Is it coincidental that, at the time of writing, one of the most popular procedures among psychotherapists is sometimes called behaviour modification? A direct outgrowth of experiments conducted by Dr. B. F. Skinner of Harvard, the treatment, in its modality and purpose, is indistinguishable from Pavlovian conditioning.

It is based upon the theory that behaviour can be changed and guided by giving or withholding desired pleasures or bodily needs. This is how it works:

When a patient responds in the "correct way" to the

behaviour pattern expected of him, he is given a reward, called by the psychiatrists, a *reinforcement*. In many mental hospitals these reinforcements are in the form of tokens which the patient may exchange for meals, permission to leave the ward (where he is obviously a prisoner), watch television or be allowed visitors.

To anyone familiar with the history of psychology, this routine is clearly a variant of the rat in a puzzle box experiment, graduated to human subjects. In the original animal studies, a rat was put into a box equipped with a small brass rod which yielded to very slight pressure and when moved downward released a small pellet of food into the tray. The rat learned to press the lever if he expected to eat. In similar experiments, cats learned to escape from "Skinner boxes" by activating a release mechanism.

Another and even more merciless man-as-animal experiment, known as ESB (for electrical stimulation of the brain) is currently in progress at several psychiatric research centres in the United States.

This intervention seeks to control human behaviour by surgically implanting micro-electrodes in certain areas of the brain and stimulating them by an electric current. Here again, a technique formerly applied only to monkeys, cats, dogs and bulls has been transferred to human subjects.

Since the brain has no feeling, when implanted with the hair-thin wires leading into even the deepest centres, brain cells respond to electrical currents or remotely controlled radio signals without the controlled individual being aware of it. He acts (or reacts) believing that he does so spontaneously and of his own free will.

"The kind of controls that can be exerted on animals and men by ESB," science writer Albert Rosenfeld tells us, "range all the way from simple muscular movements to fairly complex social behaviour."[17] (p. 97)

Trading on the public's growing fear of violence, the brain manipulators now justify their radical programme by assuring us that ESB can provide the means of controlling criminal and aggressive behaviour. The *a priori* assumption that a psychiatrist elite would have either the legal or the moral right to determine who needs such controls and to forcibly implant them is in itself an indication of how they view their role in what Floyd Matson calls "the vision of a techno-scientific future".

The psychiatrists' concern about violent behaviour is also somewhat ambivalent when one recalls that some of the most prominent spokesmen for their profession have in the past, if not condoned violence, at least explained it as being therapeutic in its effect. For example, Dr. Elliott Luby, a Detroit psychiatrist who was given a grant of $135,000 by the National Institute of Mental Health to make a study of racism, reported that the outbreaks of Negro violence were a sign of racial pride.

The disastrous Detroit riots, said Dr. Luby, were an expression of the black man's "growing identity, growing pride, growing esteem, and an indication that the black man is no longer measuring himself in terms of the white man".[18]

Others, extending the catharsis theory a step further, have encouraged and excused even murder, which was characterized as the only way the Negro could "define his manhood and achieve dignity".

Time magazine quoted psychiatrist Theodore Isaac Rubin as suggesting that a fight a day keeps the doctor away. In the *Angry Book*, according to *Time*, Dr. Rubin asks, "with a burst of earnest lyricism": "Have you ever experienced the good clean feel that comes after expressing anger, as well as the increased self-esteem, and the feel of real peace with one's self and others?"[19] (p. 32)

While Luby, Rubin *et al.* are encouraging violent behaviour, however, their colleagues are implanting electrodes in the heads of patients for the ostensible purpose of eradicating it. For instance, at an ESB clinic in Boston, one patient is a young wife whose brain is now wired for electrical stimulation because she repeatedly had fights with her husband. At last report, Dr. Frank R. Ervin, assisted by two brain surgeons, was experimenting with fifty cases of implanted brains at the Boston centre.

Similar studies are being conducted at various research centres across the U.S., notably at Tulane, Harvard and Yale Universities.

The people puppeteers have expressed an overweening self-confidence in their ability to shape and control human behaviour. Dr. James McConnell at the University of Michigan once put it this way:

"The time has come when, if you give me any normal human being and a couple of weeks – maybe a couple of months, but I don't think so – I can change his behaviour from what it is now to whatever you want it to be, if it's physically possible. I can't make him fly by flapping his wings, but I can turn him from a Christian into a Communist and vice versa."

For "scientists" who regard man as wholly animal, it is only natural that he should be a *laboratory* animal.

What kind of future, then, do these creators of a new society envision?

Ultimately, a genetically engineered, rigidly controlled race of humanoids, subject to the scientific whims of their masters in white smocks? And until that seventh day of diabolical creation arrives, a population made docile and obedient by tranquilizers, shock treatments, conditioned response, lobotomy, or electrodes in the brain?

The short answer to these terrifying questions is: yes.

In these circumstances, when L. Ron Hubbard and his adherents set out to expose the evils of psychiatry, they found ready at hand an abundance of hair-raising material.

Eschewing the polite pussyfoot prose of debating societies, the Scientologists carried forward their crusade in the hard-hitting style of political activism. From Scientology centres throughout the world issued an incessant flow of news reports, memoranda and handbills charg-

ing psychiatrists with crimes that included criminal neg-
ligence, sadistic torture, sexual assault and murder.

Specially formed organizations staged protests to direct
public attention to the charges. Groups of well-dressed,
responsible-looking youths picketed the annual meetings of
psychiatric and mental associations, carrying placards which
read: "National Association for Mental Wealth – You Fill
the Coffers, We Fill the Coffins!", "Psychiatry is
Garbage", and "Mental Health Means Money for the Brain
Butchers".

Some of the demonstrations were even more dramatic.
For example, at the 1970 annual meeting and assembly of
the National Association for Mental Health in Los Angeles,
a mime troupe, dressed in surgical gowns, staged mock
lobotomies on the pavement, using cauliflower "brains", to
protest against violent psychiatric practices.

During the annual convention of the American
Psychiatric Association in Miami, Florida, people all over
the city were startled to see an aeroplane fly overhead,
towing a row of huge letters which spelled out against the
sky the legend: PSYCHIATRY KILLS.

Scientologists cited an astonishing number of cases of
prominent or notorious persons who, after being treated by
psychiatrists, either took their own lives or committed mass
murders and assassinations. None of these had been helped
by psychiatric intervention. On the contrary, in each case
their condition had worsened during the time they had been
under the care of the specialists.

"A survey across five countries," wrote Hubbard, "failed
utterly to find *one* person who had ever been cured of
anything by psychiatrists and psychologists. The survey
found thousands who had been permanently disabled or
killed."[20] (p. 2)

The radical methods used to treat persons diagnosed as
being psychotic were also denounced by Scientology groups
dedicated to protecting the human rights of mental patients.

One of the most drastic of these procedures is that

known as lobotomy. Lobotomy is a surgical operation in which most of the connections between the frontal lobe and the rest of the brain are severed. It involves a gross destruction of tissue and results in a degeneration of a certain nucleus (called the *medialis dorsalis*) in the thalamus gland.

Hubbard has argued (with the concurrence of some psychiatrists) that not only is lobotomy destructive of brain tissue, but that it is useless as a treatment. One prominent psychiatrist had declared that "people who do lobotomy should be hanged". He added that "the fact that the procedure has fallen into ill repute does little good to the thirty or forty thousand persons who have been lobotomized in the U.S. during the last twenty years".[21]

Another, far more widely applied psychiatric treatment vehemently opposed by the Scientologists is that known as electro-convulsive therapy, abbreviated ECT. The technique involves an electric current being passed through the brain, producing violent convulsions in the patient. Dr. D. P. Sivacon, former vice-president of the World Federation for Mental Health, defined it as "a case of momentary disintegration of the personality, accompanied by important humour modifications".

Other prominent spokesmen for the profession, quoted extensively in the mass media, have repeatedly assured us that ECT is painless and extremely beneficial in the treatment of schizophrenia. "It is pleasant, harmless and extremely safe, producing no sense of shock whatever," declared one newspaper article, with snappy inaccuracy.

A patient who had been subjected to forty sessions of the therapy had this to say:

"The majority of psychiatrists and medical textbooks say that this treatment is painless ... I would say they are anything but. Imagine, if you will, lying on a couch with three or four attendants standing over you; a rubber gag is placed in your mouth (this is to keep you from chewing off your tongue during treatment); then large jolts of electricity are passed through your head, without an anaesthetic.

"These treatments cause varying degrees of memory loss for different lengths of time. It is a terrifying experience to wake up and not be able to remember your wife's name, your address, what day or what month it is or where you are. I was on the dean's list in college, in a National Honor Society fraternity (Phi Eta Sigma) and quite a good student, prior to my encounters with shock therapy. It has been about four years since my last session, and I can barely recall the names of the universities I attended, much less anything about the subject I studied . . .

"This type of therapy is not only painful but it can have a disastrous effect on the life of the patient. I think shock treatment should be eliminated from mental hospitals . . ."[22] (p. 2)

Psychiatrists who still use electro-shock treatment in what two authors have called "heroic doses", carefully avoid public statements revealing serious drawbacks in use of the therapy. They do not mention, for example, that patients have been known to break their backs during the convulsions thus induced; that some patients have been killed outright by the shock. In a recent instance of the latter kind in which electric shock treatment administered in an English mental hospital caused the death of a parish priest, a coroner recorded a verdict of "death by misadventure".[23]

Dr. Alexander John Maum Sinclair, a leading Australian psychiatrist who gave evidence against Scientology in the biased Melbourne enquiry (of which we shall speak later) described Hubbard's statements opposing ECT as "rubbish".

"I say this statement is rubbish on the basis of having personally administered something like 30 electro-shocks a week for up to eight or ten years." (That would be a total of 15,600 such interventions at the hands of this one psychiatrist!)[24] (p. 27)

Can we then classify as rubbish the statement made by Cecil and Loeb in their *Textbook of Medicine*, published in 1967: "Electro Convulsive Therapy certainly produces tissue damage in the brain and concomitant impairment of mental functions, including perception and capacity to learn."

Was Dr. Wilfred Dorfman likewise purveying rubbish when he told a Symposium on Psychiatry in 1970: "I would like to go on record as saying that electric shock treatment does produce damage to the brain and it is not only temporary"?

Perhaps the most important criticism one could make of ECT, along with other violent therapies such as brain surgery and dangerous drugs, is that they accomplish no lasting cures. Dr. Brian Inglis says as much in his book, *A History of Medicine*: "By the 1960s the gratifying rate of cures in mental hospitals, measured by the percentage of the patients considered well enough to be released was being overhauled by the readmission rate . . ."

Furthermore, it is important to have ever present in our minds what has been said concerning the lack of any exact criteria for defining mental illness. An uncounted multitude of persons are being subjected to these therapies not because they are sick, but because they are temporarily upset emotionally by every-day problems in living.

In their continuing exploration of psychiatry's twilight zone, the Scientologists have also focused public attention upon the wretched conditions which still prevail in a majority of the world's mental asylums. Labelling them "death camps", Hubbard and his followers have documented for one after another such evils as cruelty to patients, overcrowding, length of confinement, improper or inadequate medication, and commitment procedures.

In their publications and public petitions, the Scientologists have pinpointed these evils, but they have not exaggerated them. Let the reader who thinks that we have come a long day's journey from Bedlam review the reports of independent committees who have investigated contemporary psychiatric institutions.

It will suffice here to quote briefly from one such report, that describing conditions at the Chicago State Hospital and Tinley Park Center, issued May 27, 1969 by Edward V. Hanrahan, State's Attorney of Cook County, Illinois:

"Willian Bowman, aged seventy-eight, was a patient at Chicago State Hospital, partially paralyzed and confined to a wheelchair.

"On August 18, 1967, a psychiatric aide found him to be in need of a shower. She placed him in the shower while in his wheelchair, turned on the hot water valve, walked off and left him there. She did not return until approximately 1 hour and 15 minutes later. Meanwhile, a nurse's aide, hearing the shower running and seeing steam coming from the shower room, turned the water valve off and noticed the temperature had been set at 140 degrees. When she looked at Mr. Bauman she feared he was dead. The duty physician was then called to the ward. He examined Mr. Bauman, discovered him to be dead and found that he had suffered 1st, 2nd, and 3rd degree burns over the right and middle chest area and over his left thigh and lower legs and feet. The Coroner's Report shows that Mr. Bauman died from extensive burns over 30 to 35 per cent of his total body surface.

"The psychiatric aide who put Mr. Bauman in the shower returned to the scene about 1 hour and 15 minutes later. When asked why she had left her patient in the shower so long, she replied that she had an errand to run.

"During the course of our investigation, we discovered a number of other incidents involving suicide, attempted suicide, battery and rape of patients".

The outrageous state of affairs in the Chicago institution is typical of the *status quo* in similar mental wards the world over.

In Great Britain during the past five years, a whole series of scandals involving psychiatric hospitals and mental health centres have come to light, only to vanish like a London fog, having caused a little inconvenience and some

122 / *The Hidden Story of Scientology*

comment, as though they were the sort of unpleasant incidents one must expect in life.

It is difficult to shake off the suspicion that many who read newspaper accounts of the neglect, immorality and sadism experienced vicariously the same morbid interest which once prompted curious Londoners to visit Bedlam to amuse themselves by watching the behaviour of the insane patients immured there.

The contemporary scene differs only in details. Consider, by way of example, some of the findings of an official enquiry into conditions at a Lancashire mental hospital in early 1972. The Committee's report describes how "patients were locked in closets for being 'mischievous', how they were half-strangled with wet towels if they became violent, and how one victim had been injured when male nurses filled his dressing-gown pocket with alcohol and then set it afire".[25] (p. 37)

Each time new horrors were revealed, the psychiatrists in charge of the mental hospital under fire shifted responsibility to others – their subordinates or their predecessors. In all cases, their pleading was anything but persuasive; in some it was manifestly absurd.

It was absurd, for instance in a case recently uncovered in Dewsbury, England. There, a social services official discovered that two elderly women, aged seventy-four and sixty-four had been held in St. Catherine's Mental Hospital for fifty and forty-four years, respectively, even though they were sane. They had been committed to the asylum in their youth as "morally defective" because they had given birth to illegitimate children.

Psychiatrists at St. Catherine's Hospital could hardly place all the blame for this monstrous crime upon the cruel parents of these women who, together with their medical accomplices, had years ago compulsorily shut them up in a madhouse to save their relatives social embarrassment. Each psychiatric director thereafter under whose charge their incarceration continued was equally guilty.

Ralph Blakeburn, a hospital executive, denied that the women's continued detention over the years was owing to the failure of the medical authorities to review their records. He asserted that the cases were reviewed periodically and that each time the consultant psychiatrist saw the patients, he would have before him their personal information file, showing why they had been admitted in the first place. Why, then, were they not released?

The feeble excuse offered in response to this question would seem merely to compound the injustice. The women, said Blakeburn, had nowhere else they could go.

The Dewsbury scandal inevitably poses the question: how many other sane persons languish in the mental prisons of England and of the world? The number is very large; there can be no doubt about that. In addition to those who have been committed as "morally defective", there are others whose "mental illness" may have been anything from wetting the bed to public utterances against the United Nations. (The latter is an actual case which occurred in California.)

In Britain's mental wards, it has been officially estimated that one-third of the inmates are merely old people who, because of physical incapacity, are unable to care for themselves and whose families have had them committed. The same percentage is probably true of psychiatric institutions in the United States and elsewhere.

Britain's Department of Health and Social Security recently announced a plan to shut down the nation's 116 mental hospitals over the next twenty-five to thirty years, transferring the patients who really need professional care to small psychiatric units in general hospitals and eventually, when the patients are rehabilitated, to their homes. Under the plan, only those considered dangerous to themselves or to society would be confined.

The idea met with immediate opposition from members of the mental health movement. Britain's National Association for Mental Health (a WFMH affiliate) dismissed the plan as "utopian". Miss Mary Applebey, the Association's secretary, was quoted in the press as saying: "It is wishy-washy, platitudinous and dangerously superficial."[25] (p. 37)

It is also a threat to the expanding influence of the mental health elite, whose aim appears to be the increase in the number of psychiatric centres, not a decrease.

Here, as in the case of the protectionist views of medical trade unionists (among whom psychiatrists must be numbered) it is fair to ask:

Is it possible anywhere this side of the Pearly Gates for a group of people who have a vested interest in mental illness to show sincere enthusiasm for anything which promises to eliminate mental illness?

The Scientologists' whole case against psychiatry in general and the World Federation for Mental Health in particular, reduces itself to something very simple. L. Ron Hubbard states it thus:

"There is a myth that exists and is heavily promoted, that a very large percentage of the population will be in need of mental treatment at some time in their lives.

"There are many associations, trusts, groups and societies sponsored by political psychiatry and the 'best' people, who constantly repeat the message that it could be you who will need their so-called help."[26] (p. 1)

The politician appropriates hundreds of millions for institutions and community psychiatry. Promptly universities revolt, agitators flourish, crime shoots into statistics not even policemen can graph, insanity soars. This is non-delivery.

"The psychiatrist, psychologist and their clerk the sociologist, point out how bad things are getting and demand even more money. The patients who live get crazier, the state itself becomes imperilled and yet no psychiatrist or psychologist or their 'mental health' cliques ever pay back a penny of their unearned fees."[27] (p. 2)

"Various groups, including the Scientologists, objected to violence being employed in the field of mental healing and got the idea that psychiatry should be reformed. Psychiatry, reacting, got the idea that Scientology should be eradicated before it wiped out psychiatry and its millions of dollars in government 'research' grants.

"These two ideas, opposed, produced further violence by psychiatry against Scientology behind the cover of the Establishment.

"I fully agree with the idea that the psychiatric version of mental healing should not be used to bring on a '1984' as in the famous book by Orwell. Mental patients should have civil rights. They should not be beaten, tortured by strange medieval 'treatments' or killed. The women should not be raped, nor the men perverted, nor should anyone who is insane be turned into a hopeless drug addict just to make him quiet."[28]

As we have noted previously, Hubbard identified the World Federation for Mental Health, founded in 1948, as a rigidly-structured organization whose purpose was social control and world citizenship. He argued that the power and policy making of the WFMH remained in the hands of a few men whose personal backgrounds reveal radical views and subversive connections.

"The pattern of the World Federation for Mental Health is to have four or five associate groups or affiliates in a country. Only one of these is the actual working group. It usually has 'National' or 'Mental Health' as part of its title. These actual confederates collect funds and act as agents provocateurs.

"The National' in the title deludes people into thinking it is government connected and sometimes even the government is fooled. But these confederates have no more connection with the government than the main group has with the United Nations.

"By the use of these 'connections' both the confederate

and main group collect fantastic quantities of money under false pretenses.

"The organization holds 'Congresses' in various capitals yearly. These have many 'closed door' committee meetings for confederates. Russian delegates routinely attend.

"This makes a convenient meeting ground for the programmes and orders.

"Confederates come away with their briefing and go to work in their countries.

"Couriers of the main organization are continually on the move, visiting the confederates while attending the conferences of other organizations."[29] (p. 1)

The directors and supporters of WFMH and its related groups have vigorously denied Hubbard's charges and have asserted that he has deliberately misconstrued the aims and operations of the mental health movement. But to date, no responsible, independent inquiry has proved that the Scientologists have not correctly described what is inside the gift horse being offered by the mental health Trojans.

One thing is undeniably clear: psychiatry's relentless campaign against Scientology has been in part a war of revenge and in part a desperate effort to annihilate an international organization which threatens the future welfare, if not the existence, of the mental health movement.

REFERENCE NOTES

1. Thomas S. Szasz, M.D., *Ideology and Insanity*. N.Y.: 1970.
2. ———, *The Manufacture of Madness*. N.Y.: 1970.
3. Anthony M. Graziano, Ph.D., *Psychology Today*, January 1972.
4. Dr. George S. Stevenson, *Mental Health, Government and Voluntary Citizen Participation*. Address at the 15th Annual Meeting of the World Federation for Mental Health: 1962.
5. *A Brief Record of Eleven Years* – 1948–1959. Booklet published by the World Federation for Mental Health.
6. *Psychiatry*, February 1946.

7. Dr. Brock Chisholm, *The Responsibility of Psychiatry*. William Alansen White Memorial Lecture, October 23, 1945.

8. Howard P. Rome, "Psychiatry and Foreign Affairs: The Expanding Competence of Psychiatry," *The American Journal of Psychiatry*, December 1968.

9. *Mental Health and World Citizenship.* Publication of the U.S. National Association for Mental Health.

10. George S. Stevenson, M.D., *Education for Mental Health*, N.Y.: 1958.

11. William Hirsch, "Conclusions of a Psychiatrist," quoted in Dr. Albert Schweitzer's *The Psychiatric Study of Jesus*.

12. Cited in *Mental Robots*, by Lewis Albert Alesen, M.D., Caldwell, Idaho: 1957.

13. *Time* magazine, September 27, 1971.

14. *Daily Oklahoman*, March 10, 1967, cited in Dr. Thomas Szasz' *Manufacture of Madness*, p. 217.

15. Julien Cornell, *The Trial of Ezra Pound*. N.Y.: 1966.

16. *Time* magazine, June 5, 1972.

17. Albert Rosenfeld, *The Second Genesis*. N.Y.: 1969.

18. Associated Press story in the *Los Angeles Times*, March 11, 1968.

19. *Time* magazine, August 16, 1971.

20. *Freedom Scientology* (USA) No. 4: 1970.

21. Dr. Thomas S. Szasz: lecture at University of Witwatersrand University, South Africa.

22. *Freedom*, No. 24: 1970.

23. The London *Daily Telegraph*, November 18, 1969.

24. Melbourne *Truth*, June 6, 1964.

25. *Time* magazine, January 24, 1972.

26. *Freedom*, No. 24: 1970.

27. *Freedom* (USA) No. 4: 1970.

28. *Mayfair Magazine*, 1970.

29. *Freedom* No. 11: 1969.

6. *"With Evil Eye and Unequal Hand"*

When Oliver Field of AMA's Bureau of Investigation turned down the U.S. attorney's suggestion that the medical association plant a doctor-spy in the Church of Scientology, he did so because such a procedure was contrary to AMA policy.

He knew from experience that there was a better, a more effective way. In a communication to an Ohio scientist who was thirsting for Hubbard's blood, he wrote: "We notice in copies of correspondence you enclosed that Dr. Milstead of the Food and Drug Administration has indicated that investigation is going forward so far as the device the 'E-meter' is concerned, and perhaps *that activity is the only immediate hope of achieving any interference with the activities of the Scientologists.*" (Emphasis added.)

At the time Field wrote the letter just quoted, the FDA already had a secret agent named Taylor Quinn enrolled in the academy of the Founding Church of Scientology in Washington. His assignment was to entrap the Scientologists by gathering material that would purport to show that the E-meter was used to diagnose and treat disease.

In an earlier chapter, I have drawn attention to the fact that almost from the time it was set up as a federal agency, the FDA has acted as the enforcement arm of the American Medical Association. Under the guise of combatting "quackery", and using the awesome police powers of the government, FDA commissars have ruthlessly persecuted any individual or organization whose views and practices were inimical to those of orthodox medical dogma. Victims of this court-supported inquisition have included all kinds of "heretics" from lecturers on nutrition to brilliant and advanced medical researchers such as Dr. Andrew Ivy and Dr. Wilhelm Reich.

At the same time, the egregious quackery of AMA-approved psychiatry, with its fraudulent diagnoses and inhuman treatments, has been permitted to flourish.

Nothing more effectively illustrates how completely the reins of government have escaped the hands of the people in America than the operation of federal agencies such as FDA, IRS, FTC and others.

These bureaucratic hierarchies have become, in practice, sovereign rulers, with almost limitless powers to impose their will upon the people. Acting in direct conflict with America's traditional philosophy of self-rule, they combine within a single administration all three powers of government – legislative, executive and judicial. Thus, they not only make their own laws, but they interpret and enforce them. They have the power, if not the right, to indict the citizen, prosecute him before their own courts, and mete out punishment. This does not mean, however, that their despotic rule is based upon clearly established statutes or well-settled precedent cases. Instead, a defending legal counsel is faced with a huge pandect of complex, cross-indexed, vague and often *ad hoc* regulations.

Such confusion and ambiguity is not accidental. As Hannah Arendt has aptly observed: "Thus does the

9—HSOS • •

bureaucrat shun every general law, handling each situation separately by decree, because a law's inherent stability threatens to establish a permanent community in which nobody could possibly be a god because all would have to obey a law. "[1](p. 216)

Having become arrogant overlords rather than civil servants, it is inevitable that federal functionaries would be unresponsive to, when not openly contemptuous of, criticism, whether it comes from individuals, the press or even from the Congress itself.

When a Senate sub-committee was investigating FDA practices in 1965, Senator Edward V. Long, chairman, reported that FDA officials had been unco-operative, misleading and evasive. He said that throughout his committee's inquiry into the agency's activities, the one thing that stood out clearly was the rejection of any suggestion that an improvement in the bureau's procedures was called for. FDA regarded itself as above reproach.

After three full days of Senate hearings which brought to light wholesale misconduct by FDA dictocrats, Senator Long publicly reprimanded the agency in the strongest language possible. Instead of shouldering their responsibility to protect the nation's health, the committee chairman said, "We find the agency engaged in bizarre and juvenile games of cops and robbers. Instead of guarding the national health, we find an agency that is police oriented, chiefly concerned with prosecutions and convictions, totally indifferent to the individual's rights, and bent on using snooping gear to pry and invade the citizen's right of privacy."

FDA's reaction to the Senate probe was haughty disdain. An agency spokesman indicated his contempt for the proceedings when he told newsmen that witnesses who had given testimony before the committee were "well-known quacks and crackpots" (the bureaucrats' common designation for anybody who challenges their despotic rule).

When we consider this thumb-to-nose attitude of FDA

hierarchs towards a committee of the U.S. Senate, it should occasion no surprise to learn that five years later, one of Ralph Nader's study groups who scrutinized the agency's operation, found the same high-handed abuse of power and dereliction of duty.

In their published report, *The Chemical Feast*, the investigative team of seventeen students and recent graduates in the fields of medicine and law faulted the food and drug authorities for "truly massive deception" of the public and for "bureaucratic atrocities" in their enforcement procedures.

"It is fair to say," commented James S. Turner, who wrote the final report, "that none of the students expected to find in the FDA the shocking disarray and appalling failure of responsibility that their investigations revealed almost daily. As the number of altered documents, misrepresented facts and suppressed studies began to mount, the students' scepticism changed to a deep doubt about all the agency's activities, and finally ended in the conviction that most agency efforts were a failure."

The Nader research group accused FDA of expending an inordinate portion of its limited resources on "great quack campaigns", which inevitably focus on the wrong targets, such as the work of Dr. Wilhelm Reich, the health food industry and even, in the case of Scientology, on religion.

The single-minded vigour of the FDA's so-called antifraud campaign, the report added, "has led the agency into an excess of law enforcement, including the use of snooping, harrassment and prying techniques that it could not effectively defend against charges from Congress and the general public".

The "happening" which occurred at 19th and R. Streets, Washington, D.C. on the afternoon of January 4, 1963 might well have been an episode staged for the filming of a B-film about gang-busters.

Escorted by armed police on motor-cycles, two large vans pulled into the "scene", blockading the streets around the area. Several plainclothes-men got out and began moving in on the buildings at that address.

Only the sound of gunfire was missing. That was because the men with badges and guns had not surrounded a building in which dangerous criminals had holed up, ready to shoot it out with police.

They were in the act of raiding a church.

No matter what tortured legal arguments or bureaucratic sophistry are offered to justify or explain that odious incursion, the stark, simple truth must never be lost sight of:

On January 4, 1963 in Washington, a group of U.S. Marshals and deputized longshoremen, acting for an agency of the federal government, desecrated, looted and terrorized a religious centre.

That is now a historical fact.

I have included an account of that incident in two of my previous books because I regard it as an ominous milestone on the road to totalitarianism in America. Ominous because the arrogant myrmidons who perpetrated it did so with impunity; and ominous because in the long and costly legal battle which the Church has had to wage in defence of a right guaranteed by the First Amendment of the U.S. Constitution, they have fought alone.

But let us return to the scene in progress.

According to sworn affidavits of eye-witnesses and victims of the affair, the raiders charged through the main entrance beside which was a large plaque reading: FOUNDING CHURCH OF SCIENTOLOGY. In jackboot Gestapo style, they "burst into the church offices . . . and loudly if incoherently demanded and threatened all in sight; observed absolutely no courtesies except for not actually shooting the guns they carried, and denied to the Church administrators any opportunity to arrange that students and Church members not be disturbed, upset or terrorized.

"Showing no legal warrant, the agents and heavy deputies pounded their way up stairways, bursting into confessional and pastoral counselling sessions, causing disruption and violently preventing the quiet pursuit of the normal practice of religious philosophy. They broke into classrooms.

"They seized all the publications and all the confessional aids called E-meters they could find in desks, in ladies' handbags, in students' briefcases and in the session rooms."[2] (p. 11)

"Gradually, the agents removed from the church to the waiting vans some tens of thousands of copies of over twenty Church books, texts, recorded sermons; even the Church archives were sacked. The confiscated material was handled roughly, and when ministers of the Church asked that their property be handled more carefully, the 'deputies' from Baltimore gave only sneering illiteracies for answer."[3] (p. 4)

It is quite possible that the quasi-official raiders were not troubled by conscience in thus violating Church premises because the Founding Church of Scientology did not conform to the stereotype image of a place of worship – steeple, stained-glass windows, altar, pews, etc. Yet, the simple brick structure, like the earliest Quaker meeting houses of America indeed, of even the lowliest private dwelling used for religious purposes, is as inviolate under U.S. laws as the most majestic cathedral in the land.

That federal functionaries, acting in response to secret vested interests, could arrogate to themselves as they have done and daily continue to do, the right to decide matters of religious faith is but an indication of the dangerous public apathy and secular temper of our time.

What the indifferent or irreligious American public does not recognize is the fact that the primary legal principle here involved is not an attack on religion, *per se*. It is, rather, an attack on the First Amendment of the U.S. Constitution, which protects the freedom of the believer and non-believer alike and is therefore an attack on the supreme law of the nation.

During the past two decades, I have witnessed assaults not only on this pillar of American liberty, but on others as well, met with limp acquiescence by the majority of people, who speak of their cherished freedoms safeguarded by the Bill of Rights, as though such freedoms still exist. The cold-eyed fact is that despotic vandals have long since sacked and pillaged that noble edifice, which today presents to the careful observer the same picture of desolation as marble columns and crumbling pediments of the Roman Forum.

The federal judicial machinery which was intended to crush Scientology was set in motion when FDA filed in the U.S. District Court what is called a "libel of information", praying for the seizure and condemnation of the E-meter.

On the strength of that libel and without any kind of adversary hearing or prior notice of violation, Judge William B. Jones ordered a warrant to be issued. Accordingly, the court clerk issued a warrant authorizing the arrest of the meters. (The layman may wonder how the U.S. Marshals could arrest an inanimate object like an E-meter; but that is the quaint legal euphemism employed and one that in the present case concealed the fact that it was a church and its adherents who were to be the real victims of the raid.)

Although in their libel of information, the FDA did not ask for seizure or condemnation of alleged labelling – that is, literature – when the warrant was issued, it also authorized the arrest of "an undetermined number of items of written, printed or graphic matter".

In the raid on the church, which was carried out as soon as FDA officials had the warrant in their hands, federal agents seized not only the E-meters, but the entire stock of Scientology books and creedal literature. An FDA spokesman later boasted to newsmen that the agency's enforcers had seized and carted away three tons of equipment and printed material.

Why the seizure of such an enormous amount of the Church's literature when, as the District Court itself later declared, "a single false scientific, non-religious label claim is sufficient to support condemnation"?

The answer to that question is virtually self-evident: by unlawfully confiscating a large amount of the accused's property (which they hope to destroy later), the FDA dictocrats impose extra-legal punishment, no matter what the judicial outcome of the case may be.

In their accounts of the raid, newspaper reporters, whom FDA had invited to accompany the raiders, obligingly referred to the Church not as a religious organization, but as a "pseudo-scientific cult".

At a later date, *the Washington Post*, referring to the E-meters declared:

"The machines were used by the religious cult allegedly to cure a number of illnesses ranging from cancer to radiation burns from atomic bombs, according to testimony at the trial."[7] The story did not venture to estimate how many Scientologists were survivors of a nuclear war.

Such a lapse in objective reporting is, of course, not at all unusual. In today's media, the naked truth is as rare as a naked nun (perhaps in our time, even rarer).

FDA officials were fully aware, and the press should have been, that the Founding Church of Scientology had been duly incorporated on July 21, 1955 as a non-profit society and corporation under the laws of the District of Columbia.

The Church's Creed, the body of doctrinal literature swept up by the raiders (and later filed by government lawyers as exhibits) make it plain to any reasonable person that Scientology is a religion.

Motions by the Scientology lawyers to have the FDA action quashed on the grounds that it violated both the First and the Fourth Amendments were denied, first by

District Judge Luther W. Youngdahl and later (on a motion limited to written material) by District Judge Edward A. Tamm.

Four years ensued before the FDA charges were heard in court. When the case was finally brought to trial on April 3, 1967, the federal agency still maintained the fiction that they were not taking legal action against a Church. It was that bad old E-meter that was the defendant of record.

According to FDA's complaint, the labelling for the meter (a term used to designate the whole range of Scientology literature) contained statements which "represent, suggest or imply" that the E-meter was adequate and effective for diagnosis, prevention, treatment, detection and elimination of a long list of human diseases, including arthritis, cancer, stomach ulcers and radiation from atomic bombs.

All of which was a monstrous lie. Nowhere in any Scientology publication was it ever remotely hinted that the E-meter could be used to treat anything. As delineated in a previous chapter, the instrument was developed to measure the intensity of facsimiles or mental-image pictures of past incidents during some stages in the process of auditing. As such, the meter is clearly a confessional aid and has never been used by ministers of the Church in any other way.

Nevertheless, the first trial resulted in a general jury verdict for the government, and District Judge John J. Sirica ordered destruction of the seized E-meters, together with a quantity of the printed material.

Attorneys for the Church immediately appealed the case, arguing that the E-meters were used only as part of a religious practice, to audit and process the mental and spiritual condition of adherents. Auditing was conducted within the church and anyone entering was on notice that it was a church. "It had a sign on the door, there is a chapel, there was a Sunday School; we married people, we had funerals."

To make sure that applicants for auditing understood

that the procedure took place within a spiritual context, they were required to sign a release which stated in part:

"I understand fully and completely that the said purpose of said organizations and employed personnel, is based upon the practice of Scientology which I know to be a spiritual and religious guide intended to make persons more aware of themselves as spiritual beings, and not treating or diagnosing human ailments of body or mind, and not engaged in the teachings of medical arts or sciences . . ."

Anyone who was ill, declared the Scientologists, was referred to a medical doctor. If a person seeking help from Scientology appeared to be seriously ill, he was refused auditing until he did consult a physician and had his condition diagnosed and treated.

"Against this background," argued the Church's legal spokesmen, "it is impossible to say that the E-meter is intended for healing purposes, regardless of what impression might be gained from an isolated reading of literature."

In a two to one decision, the U.S. Court of Appeals reversed the lower court's verdict, ruling that the Founding Church of Scientology was indeed a bona fide religious organization.

The Government, said the High Court's majority opinion, erred in 1963 when it confiscated the Church's E-meters, which were used "to diagnose the mental and spiritual condition" of a subject.

The court also noted that the alleged labelling of the E-meters "is not a single readily digestible book or a collection of pamphlets obviously promotional in nature, but rather a vast array of the often obscure literature of Scientology".

Writing the majority opinion, Judge J. Skelly Wright said that accounts of auditing, integrated into the general theory of Scientology are *prima facie* religious doctines, and that "literature setting forth religious doctrines, and related to an instrument in the manner in which the 'auditing' literature here is related to the E-meter, cannot be subjected to courtroom evaluation and therefore cannot be considered 'labelling' of such an instrument for purposes of the 'false or mislabelling' provisions of the Act" (under which FDA had moved against the instruments).

Even though FDA thus stood judicially adjusted as having acted illegally in seizing equipment and scriptural literature protected by the Constitution, the federal apparachiki were not ready to accept the appeal court's ruling and throw in the sponge. Instead, they filed a petitition for a rehearing.

Despite the straightforward, lucid opinion just cited, clearly stating that the Food and Drug Administration was seeking to interfere in religious matters that lay outside its purview, the appeal court granted the government's petitition for a rehearing of the case.

Not only that, but the court now "clarified" its ruling, stating that "we found that *some* of the literature was at least *prima facie* religious doctrine". It suggested that on retrying the case, the District Court should make an item-by-item determination of whether any item of Scientology literature put forth claims on a wholly non-religious basis or whether a religious appeal "has been merely tacked on" to any item.

The District Court refused to do any such thing. Noting that the seized literature contained some 20,000 pages, the trial court said that a single false scientific non-religious label claim was sufficient to support FDA's charges.

Defence attorneys, asserting that the most salient feature of the case at bar was the fact that Scientology is a religion, argued that the government had to prove by clear and convincing evidence that the religious practice of auditing was one of the gravest abuses, endangering paramount interest.

But the appeal court, in reversing the findings of the first trial, had already declared:

"Here the E-meter has been condemned, not because it is itself harmful, but because the representations made concerning it are 'false and misleading'. And the largest part of those representations is contained in the literature of Scientology describing the process of auditing which appellants have claimed, without contest from the Government, is part of their religion and central to its exercise."[6]

The Government had used the misbranded device charge merely as a handle to institute the legal action, said the Scientology lawyers. "But the entire thrust of their case is directed against spiritual healing and improvement. Without the books and pamphlets referring to auditing, the Government is left with a completely harmless article, a variation of which can be purchased in a toy shop.

"The entire Government argument that the 'unthinking' public needs the protection of the Food and Drug Administration when they go to confession is a ridiculous, unconstitutional and 'unthinking' extension of Government paternalism."

The defence also argued that in the government's singling out the Church of Scientology's religious use of an artifact, from the many religions in U.S. which also use artifacts, was establishment of religion, prohibited by the establishment clause of the First Amendment.

Other religions, without interference from the Government, "buy, sell, and transport in interstate commerce articles and literature concerning and making health claims for such articles.

"These articles, used by other religions, are stated to have healing powers. A partial catalogue of these articles stated to have healing power for which health claims are made would include the Roman Catholic use of the Lourdes Water, Holy Water, Easter Wafer, Scapulars (cloth straps), Saint Glaize Candles for healing and preventing throat disease, Miraculous Medals. Similarly the Fundamentalists faith healers use Prayer Cloths, oil, and red pieces of string, for which healing claims are made."

The Scientologists cited legal precedent to show that the Government must be neutral when it comes to religious organizations. To do otherwise was discriminatory and a denial of equal protection of the law. In a previous case (*Yick Wo v. Hopkins* 118 U.S. 356), a federal court had stated:

"Though the law itself be fair on its face and impartial in appearance, yet, if it is applied and administered by public authority with an evil eye and unequal hand, so as practically to make unjust and illegal discrimination between persons in similar circumstances, material to their rights, the denial of equal justice is still within the prohibition of the Constitution."

The Government presented no new evidence at the second trial.

Once again, however, the District Court found in favour of the government and entered an order condemning the meters and all the confiscated writings. And once again, on November 24, 1971, attorneys for the Church filed notice of appeal.

Like all legal battles between the Government goliath and the private sector, the contest was greatly uneven. The protracted litigation was costing the defendants a great deal of money, which they would never be able to recover, no matter what the outcome of the preceedings.

The federal dictocrats, on the other hand, had available to them the limitless financial resources of the national treasury – that is to say, the people's money. They had spent thousands of dollars prosecuting a minority religion for employing a simple galvanometer in its practice, an instrument which the District Court itself had declared to be harmless, adding that destruction of it would intrude upon religion. The only possible loser on their side of the bar was the taxpayer.

In a brief filed with the U.S. Court of Appeals following the second trial in the District Court, lawyers for the Church of Scientology again argued that the "misbranded device" provisions of the federal Food, Drug and Cosmetic Act were not applicable to a harmless instrument such as the E-meter, which is central to a bona fide religious practice.

Under First Amendment guarantees of religious freedom, it was a well-settled fact of law that such an encroachment could be justified only in cases that involved the gravest abuses which endangered paramount interests.

Even then, a regulation of religious practice is invalid unless the Government can show "that no alternative forms of regulation would combat such abuses without infringing First Amendment rights".[4]

The FDA was trying to apply a consumerism statute to matters of religion by attempting to prove the "misbranding" of a confessional aid because its "labelling" – that is, the Church's scripture – did not bear adequate directions for its use!

Who gave the food and drug mandarins the right to determine what are or are not adequate directions for the use of a harmless galvanometer used in a religious setting?

"If there is any fixed star in our constitutional constellation," declared the Supreme Court in an earlier case, "it is that no official, high or petty, can prescribe what shall be orthodox in politics, nationalism, religion or other matters of opinion or force citizens to confess by word or act their faith therein."[5]

That constitutional luminary may still be shining steadfastly out there in the legal firmament somewhere, but it has long since been lost to the view of federal agencies, such as FDA and IRS, who daily issue official opinions on virtually every act of the citizen's life, including religious acts. And their officially proclaimed dogma has, time after time, been supported by the nation's courts. It was the Supreme Court itself that in 1954 declared that the state may set up standards that are "spiritual as well as physical, aesthetic as well as monetary".

Dangerous and chilling words these, coming from the court of last resort. As in the case of so many other decisions that have followed in the past two decades, the cynical observation of Chief Justice Marshall that the Constitution means what the judges say it means, would seem to apply. Indeed, the U.S. today is ruled not by law, but by judges, some of whom grossly distort or wholly ignore the clear meaning of the supreme statutes. The result has been a gradual erosion of public respect for the entire legal system in America.

When the U.S. Court of Appeals issued a final ruling in its "clarified" rehearing of the Scientology case, the three-judge panel again reaffirmed the judgment of the District Court, and ordered the FDA to return to the Church of Scientology the literature and E-Meters seized in the illegal 1962 raid.

This judgment was widely interpreted in the press and elsewhere as a great victory in the church's fight for religious freedom. As the large truck drew up in front of the Founding Church of Scientology in Washington to return the material the Government had confiscated in its Nazi-style raid more than nine years previously, a large crowd of onlookers burst into loud applause. The Scientologists themselves celebrated with ceremony and champagne the seemingly successful denouement of the longest case ever brought by the FDA.

However, a careful look at the legal facts makes it abundantly clear that the church's adherents were celebrating something less than a Pyrrhic victory.

While directing the FDA to return the confiscated material, the high court at the same time ordered the Scientologists to pay the enormous storage bill for warehousing the literature and devices stolen and held by the FDA for so long.

Not only that, but the church was also required to pay all legal costs and fees of the Government's disgraceful prosecution of them (exclusive of those involved in their appeal following the first trial.)

The judges further decreed that the Scientologists must

post a penal bond of $20,000 to insure their compliance with the court's judgment.

Yet another clause of the court's ruling restored the master-slave relationship between FDA and the church by making the E-meter and credal literature subject to provisions of the Federal Food, Drug and Cosmetic Act. Even worse, it stated that "the Founding Church of Scientology of Washington, D.C., Inc., shall compensate the United States of America for costs of reasonable supervision of matters under the direction or control of the Church at the rate of $8.00 per hour, per representative for each hour or portion thereof actually employed in such supervision under the terms of this Decree as salary or wage; and where subsistence expenses are incurred, at the rate of $25.00 per day or portion thereof per person for such subsistence expenses. Said claimant shall also compensate the United States of America (i.e., FDA commissars) for necessary traveling expenses and for any other necessary expenses which may be incurred in connection with supervisory responsibilities of the United States Food and Drug Administration."

Most shocking of all the judges' over-riding contempt for the Bill of Rights in purporting to exercise prior restraint in the publication of the churches literature: "Any and all items of written, printed, or graphic matter which directly or indirectly refers to the E-meter or to Dianetics and/or Scientology and/or auditing or processing shall not be further used or distributed unless and until" the said items carried a printed caveat on the outside front cover or in the title page, a "warning" prescribed by FDA.

In these circumstances, the Church of Scientology's long and costly legal battle against governmental despotism assumes an importance far beyond its own self-interest.

All Americans, whether religiously affiliated or not, were the unnamed defendants in the case.

(Reference Notes will be found on page 233)

7. *The Little Gods Down Under*

The U.S. Food and Drug Administration's move against Scientology did not deal the crippling blow to the movement that its initiators had hoped it might do.

Confiscation of the Church's E-meters occasioned a brief period of inconvenience; the court trials entailed a substantial outlay for legal fees and provided material for biased news stories in the media; but Scientology was growing faster than ever.

Not only in America, but in other English-speaking countries as well, people in great numbers were enrolling in communications courses and auditing sessions. A man-and-wife team of hack writers who had been put to work to do a derogatory magazine piece on the movement, lamented: "Millions of young people all over the world are becoming 'addicted' to the dangerous new cult of Scientology."

News of the FDA raid, always in a slanted and sometimes in a distorted version, was given the widest circulation possible, in an effort to discredit Scientology abroad. The global network of Scientology's detractors correctly reasoned that the prestige of the U.S. Government would lend weight to their charges that Hubbard and his adherents were operating what an AMA official called "a well organized piece of chicanery".

In Australia, where Scientology had attracted a very large following, the much-publicized FDA action encouraged the Church's enemies to renew their attacks with even greater vigour.

The best organized and loudest campaign was mounted in the state of Victoria, where Scientologists had the largest and most active branches.

Unlike the Church's opponents in the United States, who remained discreetly in the background and used other persons and organizations to do their fighting for them, the Australian group made no bones about identifying themselves. It was composed of prominent psychiatrists, psychologists, professors from Melbourne University, mental health crusaders, members of the Australian Medical Association and their obedient representatives, the civil authorities.

Leading the pack was Dr. E. Cunningham Dax, chairman of the Victoria Mental Health Authority. In 1962, he wrote to every Minister of Health in Australia, citing what he considered to be the dangers of Scientology. He also urged the State Government to curb the activities of Scientologists by prohibiting their advertising.

An interesting fact about Dr. Dax is that he attended the inaugural congress of the World Federation for Mental Health in 1948, and has maintained close ties with that organization over the ensuing years. In 1961, the WFMH sponsored the publication of Dr. Dax's book, *Asylum To Community*, which describes the rapid expansion of community psychiatric centres in Australia.

As elsewhere in the world, the enemies of Scientology found willing allies in the press. One of Melbourne's leading dailies, curiously named *Truth*, boasted in its news columns that the paper had "spearheaded the initial

10—HSOS • •

onslaught against Scientology in the early 1960s".[1] (p. 13)

No pretence of objective reporting was made by any of the Australian media. The usual "eminent critics" of Scientology – spokesmen for the Australian Medical Association, health authorities and leading psychiatrists – were accorded front-page prominence as they daily voiced their deep concern about the dangers of Scientology. Lengthy commentaries on previously published reports of the U.S. marshals' raid on Scientology's Washington headquarters continued to appear, with not a single line of explanation or rebuttal from the Scientologists. The newspaper accounts carefully avoided mention of the fact that the U.S. authorities had, in fact, raided a church. Instead, the stories stated that the marshals had "raided the headquarters of the Academy of Scientology". This secular designation was more in keeping with the establishment thesis that L. Ron Hubbard was a mental-health quack, preying upon "thousands of neurotics in Melbourne, in desperate need of proper medical care", that is to say, people who should be swelling the ranks of "patients" attending the proliferating psychiatric clinics and outpatient departments set up by the Mental Hygiene Service. *Truth*, the Melbourne newspaper mentioned in a foregoing paragraph, consistently referred to Scientology as "bunkumology".

The biased handling of news is effectively illustrated by the comparative "play" given a call for evidence against Scientology, and the lack of response to that appeal.

Noting that the Government was powerless to move against Scientologists until they had valid evidence, to support such a move, Victorian Health Minister R. W. Mack issued a statement asking people who thought they had proof of illegal practices by Scientologists to contact the Crown Law Department.

The health official's request for information about alleged exploitation by Scientologists was given major prominence in the newspapers and run under a three-column, three-bank headline.

When not a single person came forward with a complaint against Scientology, the no-response story was a brief three-paragraph item, buried beneath an 18-point, one-column head. (I am here referring to articles in the *Melbourne Age* of August 10 and 14, 1963, respectively, which were typical.)

For more than two years, at the instigation of Scientology's "eminent critics", both the police department and investigators for Victoria's Department of Health had subjected the Church's activities to intensive investigation. But, according to a public statement of the Minister for Health, the authorities could find nothing in existing laws under which the Scientologists could be prosecuted.

New legislation would have to be drafted to stop them. That called for fancy footwork on the political level. Accordingly, a plan of action was worked out. Phillip Bennett Wearne, a disgruntled former Scientologist, acted as front man for the get-Scientology alliance. In his own words:

"I knew that the way to go about it was to go to the Labour Opposition; so former political contacts put me in touch with the Hon. J. Walton, M.L.C., and he was most interested in bringing in the subject. He was a back-bencher, and a successful attack on some subject like this would be very helpful to his career as a politician. So I made several visits to Parliament and he recorded conversations about it, and I gave him notes and documents, and one thing and another."[2] (p. 2)

On October 17, 1963, Walton delivered an anti-Scientology speech in the Victorian Legislative Council, calling for a full governmental inquiry into the practices of the dangerous cult.

His remarks were prominently quoted in the press.

Perceiving that the Opposition had hold of a good thing, John W. Galbally, Labour leader in the Upper House, gave the attack on Scientology his personal attention. In a high-decibel speech before the Legislative Council, Galbally censured the Government for its failure to deal with the wicked "cult", despite repeated warnings from the Mental Hygiene Authority "and other responsible persons and bodies" (meaning mental health lobbyists and the AMA).

Availing himself of parliamentary privilege, which protected him against charges of slander, he described Scientologists as charlatans who were guilty of intimidation and blackmail, which could lead to insanity and even suicide.

Then, evidently in the belief that to deliver a truly rousing political oration, one must, in the words of former President Johnson, "get your hand up *under* the dress", Galbally read from a list of questions he said were asked of Scientology "victims who underwent lie detector tests". He came down hard on those having to do with sexual acts and perversions.

In its sensationalized coverage of the speech, the *Melbourne Truth* modestly refused to cite any of the questions which, it said, any newspaper "conscious of public decency would not publish."

"It is a scandal," Galbally declared, "that the Government allows this sort of thing to go on in Melbourne."

The Labour Leader's words were still ringing in the air when his colleague, J. M. Walton, rose to continue the onslaught. From his briefcase he produced an E-meter, the harmless device that had figured in the now-famous FDA raid on the Founding Church of Scientology in Washington.

"This is the instrument the Scientologists use to extract confessions from people in prominent places in the community," he told House members.

He added dramatically: "We are dealing with something that is very deep and very dangerous."

He was, in fact, dealing with a simple skin galvanometer, but the Victorian MPs had never seen one before and were properly impressed.

In a final, thumb-screw tactic, Walton suggested that perhaps some members of the Government had themselves been consorting with Scientologists, to whom they had divulged their secrets. Because of this they had used their influence to prevent any official action against the cult.

Yielding to the combined pressure of Opposition political leaders and mental health lobbyists, the Victorian Governor-in-Council on November 27, 1963 appointed a Board of Inquiry to "inquire into, report upon, and make recommendations concerning Scientology as known, carried on, practised and applied in Victoria".

The "Board" consisted of one man – Kevin Victor Anderson, Q.C., a senior member of the Victorian Bar and a practicing Roman Catholic. Appointed counsel to assist the Board in conducting the Inquiry was Gordon Just, instructed by the Crown Solicitor.

The marathon Inquiry set something of a record for such proceedings, both in terms of the time consumed (160 days of sittings) and the enormous bulk of testimony (nearly 4,000,000 words, which filled 8,920 pages of transcript).

When the Inquiry was first announced, the Scientologists expressed enthusiasm for the hearings because, they said, such an impartial review of the evidence would completely vindicate Scientology. They co-operated fully with the Board, providing all documents and records that were requested.

As the Inquiry went forward, however, the proceedings appeared more and more like an adversary situation in which they were defendants. In a later legal brief, their lawyers said: "The Inquiry into Scientology was not judicial in constitution, it was not judicial in function and only perhaps in its 'trappings' was it superficially judicial in its procedure."

A careful, unbiased reading of the transcript certainly supports some of the principal charges made by the Scientologists against the Inquiry; for example, that Anderson sometimes adopted the role of prosecutor, and harried both witnesses and counsel for Scientology, while treating with courtesy and deference those "expert" witnesses hostile to Scientology; that there was collusion among anti-Scientology witnesses; that the Board declared some findings before all the witnesses were heard; and that Anderson and Just used confidential information from Scientology files to embarrass and ridicule witnesses for Scientology.

Sessions of the Inquiry that were heard *in camera* sometimes bore a striking resemblance to the witch trials of the fifteenth and sixteenth centuries. It is only necessary to identify sex as the Devil and Scientologists as the witches who cor sort with him. An auditing session here figures in the same way as Sabbats of the past.

The transcript of these sittings was issued as a secret appendix to the published report and was not generally circulated. However, I have come into possession of a copy and will quote a portion of it to show the inquisitional nature of the proceedings.

The date of this hearing was September 18, 1964 and the Board's counsel, Gordon Just, was leading the evidence. The witness being interrogated was a Scientology staff member.

"MR. JUST: If the Board pleases: I am going to put some material to Mrs. Williams which people with ears unaccustomed to obscene language and the like would perhaps best not remain to hear. It is the sort of language which would not be, I think, normally used in most places, but I propose to put it to Mrs. Williams – language used on the files as recorded by various people.

THE BOARD: Very well.

MR. JUST: Mrs. Williams, when you are auditing a male preclear does it embarrass you if that man starts talking about cunts?

WITNESS: I would not attach any particular significance to it.

MR. JUST: I am not going to have any naming of the preclear in question, but on a file (perhaps Mr. Crook may write the name of the file down and hand it into the Board and my friend) of a male preclear, when you were yourself the auditor, this appears: Auditor's report forms, then the preclear's name. I think it is fair to say it was a staff member – a staff co-auditor. Question: what question shouldn't I ask you? Then there is a note about the tone arm: what sexual activity could you confront, not confront: havingness: point about something. What question shouldn't I ask you? Then 4-T-A havingness 3-T-A. Then on Pre-Session Comm. – there is written on this, O.W.'s a word I cannot now read, but you may know it, Mrs. Williams. I think it is your writing. Then the word fannys (cunts): further down, what terminals are unflat on case: fanny/cunt: auditor's opinion on progress: ran incident on being a nun in 1643 name Isabel, main point of attention fixed on (cunts), ran incident on what question shouldn't I ask you: got T.A. reading proper. Is that your writing? (Document shown to witness).

WITNESS: Yes.

MR. JUST: What is the word I could not read there, perhaps you would read it; it is half way down the page?

WITNESS: O.W.'s oh, I think that is 'nuns'.

MR. JUST: That may well be. You were not embarrassed or shocked by this sort of language?

WITNESS: Not really, no.

MR. JUST: Coming from a male in an auditing session?

WITNESS: Well, as an auditor I have been trained to listen without showing anything, or that sort of thing.

THE BOARD: Do you frequently come across this?

WITNESS: No.

BOARD: You were not prepared for this sort of thing?

WITNESS: Well, not frequently, I have heard sometimes.

BOARD: From time to time?

WITNESS: Yes.

BOARD: Not from any preclear, this is by no means an exceptional case?

WITNESS: No, from time to time –

BOARD: So that you were quite accustomed to this sort of language and this sort of discussion taking place between the preclear and yourself?

WITNESS: No, I am not accustomed to it.

BOARD: I mean by 'accustomed' it occurs from time to time and such occurrences do not occasion you any surprise?

WITNESS: Well, again, one is trained to listen.

BOARD: What is the answer to my question?

WITNESS: I am sorry.

BOARD: Does it happen from time to time with such frequency that this occurrence does not occasion you any surprise?

WITNESS: No, it doesn't.

BOARD: It doesn't occasion you any surprise?

WITNESS: No, it doesn't happen a lot.

BOARD: I think we have our negatives crossed. When it happens, you are not surprised it happens?

WITNESS: No.

BOARD: You are not surprised?

WITNESS: M'mm.

MR. JUST: With this same member of the staff, 26th October 1960, Auditor's Report Forms: Terminals assessed today: sexual organs. Then amongst other things: Auditor's opinion on progress: PC has chronic PTP on sex organs. (Then I think what follows does not add to the case very much.) [By the latter statement, Counsel probably meant there was nothing of a titillating nature in the intervening portion of the file.] That did not surprise you – a male preclear: terminals assessed today: 'Sexual organs'?

WITNESS: No. When one assesses cases, if it reads on the meter and has charge on it, that is, if the T.A. moves on it – the tone arm on the meter moves up and down on it – it would have some bearing on the case and that is what would be audited.

BOARD: Can you tell from either of those that Mr. Just has spoken to you about, how long the processing session took on the particular topics that have been mentioned.

WITNESS: M'mmm.

MR. JUST: His answers would be frank answers, discussing all sorts of sexual behaviour, would they?

WITNESS: I imagine they would be.

BOARD: How old was this preclear at this stage?

WITNESS: Forty or something.

BOARD: Married to your knowledge?

WITNESS: Married.

BOARD: You were twenty-four at that stage, were you – four years ago?

WITNESS: Yes.

MR. JUST: How old was [name omitted], the auditor?

WITNESS: I think she'd be about twenty-two now.

MR. JUST: That makes her, in February 1962, somewhere about twenty, and on this same preclear, on February 26th, 1962, on the 'Results and Comments' column the note is: 'All the sexy things we came up with in the last intensive, January '62.' That rather indicates that this young auditor on that occasion was subject to talking about all the sexy things this particular preclear may have been interested in at the time?

WITNESS: If it had a charge on it, that would definitely be audited."

The interrogation continues in this vein, *ad nauseam*; but I will spare the reader. It is not necessary to eat a whole egg to know that it's rotten.

From the foregoing, it is clear, I think, that for Anderson and Just, mention of repressed sexual feelings and recall of past incidents, even within the context of pastoral counselling, was shocking, shameful and wrong. It went against the grain of the two men's upringing, their social, moral and religious outlook.

Scientologists who were present report that sometimes during testimony which explained beliefs and practices of Scientology, Anderson was heard to mutter unjudiciously, "Rubbish!" and "Nonsense!" These remarks were not recorded in the transcript.

Among the witnesses hostile to Scientology, two were outstanding because of the quality and extent of their testimony.

The first of these was Dr. E. Cunningham Dax, chairman of Victoria's Mental Health Authority and long-time active member of the World Federation for Mental Health. Speaking from on high, Dr. Dax defined the objectives of Scientology as indoctrination of a large number of blind, uncritical and faithful followers, who were trained to spread Scientology principles in order to satisfy their leader's lust for power. He said an alleged IQ test form used by Scientologists to test a person's intelligence quotient included matters of personality, intelligence and sometimes mental disturbance which would be impossible to measure with accuracy in the way it purported to do.

With regard to the E-meter, Dr. Dax testified that it had been used in the United States as a lie-detector and was an instrument not employed in normal psychiatric practice. Grave doubts about it had been raised in America. He added that the fact that the person being "audited" knew he had disclosed some of his innermost secrets to an organization might have a dangerous effect on him. A person who had confessed would often wish he could get the information back, but he could not recover the material. "I am convinced this is enough to induce ill-health, chronic anxiety and psychosomatic symptoms in people who had expressed their shortcomings."

Reaching somewhat far afield for symptoms, Dr. Dax suggested that a guilt feeling had prompted L. Ron

Hubbard to call the 1962 Scientology meeting in Australia the "Clean Hands congress". Washing the hands, he explained, was commonly associated with feelings of guilt.

After admitting that he had never met L. Ron Hubbard, nor, indeed, ever set eyes on him, Dax proceeded to practise the kind of remote diagnosis common to his profession, and pronounced the founder of Scientology to be a person of unsound mind, suffering from paranoid schizophrenia.

Various Scientology writings supported this view, he assured the Board of Inquiry. "They display all sorts of exhibitions of histrionics and are hysterical."

The second and even more prolific witness against Scientology who deserves special attention was Phillip Wearne, executive officer of the Committee for Mental Health and National Security. His testimony, comments and questions fill a massive 348 pages of transcript – enough to make an average-size book.

Wearne first appeared before the Inquiry as a witness vehemently opposed to Scientology and whose references to it were couched in the most intemperate language used during the entire course of the hearings. His remarks were studded with terms such as corpse, creature, un-person, nasty child, beast, imbecile, monkey, zombie, and so on. Typical references to Scientologists:

"You get the impression that the exterior entity cleverly keeps the pupils of the eyes fixed in a suitable direction while the mouth talks."

"Its eyes move like the eyes of a living person."

"This creature is, by all human standards, inside out."

"The remains of the former personality at some moments speak through the lips of the un-person."

It was after a lengthy address of this kind that the Board – Mr. Anderson – said:

"Thank you, Mr. Wearne; I am greatly obliged to you for your thorough, very complete and very painstakingly prepared and delivered address. It speaks volumes for the amount of labour and tremendous industry you have applied to the preparation of your case."

When the Counsel who represented the Committee for Mental Health and National Security withdrew during the protracted Inquiry, Wearne asked the Board for permission to represent the committee himself. Anderson granted this request and invited Wearne to sit at the Bar table, where he asked questions, led evidence and cross-examined witnesses.

In a lengthy statement, in the form of an affidavit sworn to before a notary some time after the Anderson board closed its Inquiry, Wearne related in detail the circumstances surrounding his participation in the Inquiry proceedings.

He said that one day prior to the Inquiry he was discussing Scientology with his bank manager, who suggested that he get in touch with Dr. E. Cunningham Dax, chairman of Victoria's Mental Hygiene Authority.

"I met Dr. Dax and explained to him my hostility to Scientology. It was obvious to me he didn't know anything about Scientology, and he could not relate it to any of the psychological or psychiatric disciplines because he did not have any of the necessary lexicon of terms. He did not have the Rosetta stone, so to speak, to translate Scientology into psychological terms and show it up to be a perverted form of psychology.

"It was equally clear to me that he was extremely antagonistic to Scientology and wished its destruction and saw me as a means of accomplishing it. This became even more evident throughout the Inquiry when Dax gave his evidence on the basis of the research and material which I had provided, which material I had extracted in part from his psychiatric library and which he had been so willing to study in the publications which I distributed, such as *Probe*."

Wearne gathered together a handful of former Scientologists whom he carefully briefed to give evidence before the Board of Inquiry. On the whole their testimony appears to me to be unconvincing and ambiguous.

One of the witnesses, a man named Douglas Moon, went on about it for 511 pages, but at times no one, including Moon himself, apparently knew what he was talking about.

Throughout the Melbourne hearings, a mysterious observer haunted the proceedings, a man Wearne tentatively identified as an agent for CIA.

"Now this chappie," said Wearne, "appeared about the second day of the Board of Inquiry and was a constant shadow – you know – if you looked around at any time of the day, you would find him there; and he was always approaching me and talking to me about the Inquiry and how it was going and what the witnesses were doing and how they should be handled and so on. He didn't know what he was talking about, really – but as he insisted on inviting me for lunch practically daily, I felt obliged to listen to him anyway.

"He made it his business to keep in close contact with me. I became embarrassed by the number of times that he wined and dined me, brought liquor to my flat and irritated me by constant and inept suggestions concerning Scientology witnesses. On one occasion, Doug Moon, who considered him an intolerable ratbag, when probed by him as to what evidence he would give, abused him in tones of high anger and left the flat, slamming the door behind him.

"I was tolerant because, while I realised he did not have a clue about how our programme against Scientology should be conducted, he was trying to do his best and I assume was being paid for it. If I remember rightly, I made him a member of the Committee for Mental Health and National Security and gave him a card which no doubt is held in a repository of honour in his archives either at the CIA office or whoever else was paying him.

"I rather prefer the idea that the security service that employed him was the CIA because both he and his brother-in-law were employed in a finance company which had a set of offices to the rear of the United States Consulate, an organization which I approached at one time to interview the CIA man in charge."

Hubbard himself did not appear to give testimony before the Board, a fact which is dwelt upon at some length by the Anderson Report. The report does not mention, however, that solicitors for the Scientology organization in Melbourne on September 28, 1964, formally requested that the state of Victoria pay Hubbard's travelling and incidental expenses to fly to Australia from England to give evidence.

The request was refused, as was a proposal that the Board appoint some representative in England to hear evidence from Hubbard there.

Regarding the latter suggestion, Anderson said that such evidence taken on Commission was a very poor substitute for actual oral evidence before a tribunal. "One has to see the witnesses, observe their demeanour. In fact, one has to see whether they are 'Dear Alice-ing' you to determine whether what they are saying are things you, as a tribunal, should accept. I feel that I could get no assistance from Mr. Hubbard's evidence if all I had before me was his evidence taken on Commission. It would only be the bald written word without any means available of appraising the demeanour of the witness and those other multitude of things which one's professional training and years of life, for that matter, enable one to form some fair appraisal of the weight which would be given to the evidence."

While thus refusing to consider evidence in the form of interrogatories put to Hubbard by an experienced lawyer in England, Anderson based his eventual findings upon what he called "the great body of scientific evidence... experts in a variety of fields, scientific and otherwise". That is, he relied upon psychiatrists, doctors, lawyers, university professors and others, most of whom had never come closer to Scientology than the "bald written word", here declared to be so unsatisfactory.

Critics of Scientology and its founder have said that Hubbard had had no intention of coming to Melbourne; that the request for expense money had been made, knowing that it would be rejected.

If true, it merely shows that Hubbard was using good sense. Only four months prior to the request, Dr. E. Cunningham Dax, chairman of the Mental Health Authority in Victoria, had publicly declared Hubbard to be of unsound mind. There was open discussion among the legal profession that he could now be charged with fraud.

Gordon Just, Counsel assisting the Board had reportedly said that "the people" of Victoria were so irate against Hubbard that they might do him physical injury if he were available. When the Scientologists' lawyer asked that the authorities guarantee Hubbard's personal safety, Just replied that this could not be done because it would interfere with the ordinary workings of the law.

The newspapers were treating the Inquiry with the kind of biased sensationalism usually reserved for an especially gruesome murder trial. There is no need here to quote from the fulsome stories that dominated the Melbourne dailies during the hearings. A few randomly selected headlines and banners will suffice to indicate the tone and slant of the coverage:

"SCIENTOLOGY IS PERVERTED"[3] (p. 4)
"[SECURITY] CHECK A FORM OF BLACKMAIL"[4] (p. 3)
"SCIENTOLOGY CAUSED 'DELUSIONS' "[5] (p. 29)
"SCIENTOLOGY 'EXPLOITED ANXIETY' "[6] (p. 23)
"SCIENTOLOGY IS A MENACE"[7] (p. 5)
"PRODUCT OF AN UNSOUND MIND"[8] (p. 2)

There can be little doubt that, given the climate of opinion which then prevailed in Victoria, Hubbard would have been certified as insane or jailed for fraud if he had set foot within the jurisdiction of his enemies.

The Board of Inquiry concluded its hearing on April 21, 1965 and Anderson tabled his report in Parliament the first week in October of the same year. In his report, Anderson attacked Scientology in what one news account called "the strongest terms ever used in an official investigation in Australia".

In the summary of his findings, Anderson denounced Scientology *in toto*. "The Board has been unable to find any worthwhile redeeming feature in Scientology." The whole body of its doctrine was a "fabric of falsehood, fraud and fantasy".

"Scientology is evil; its techniques evil, its practice a serious threat to the community, medically, morally and socially; and its adherents sadly deluded and often mentally ill."

As for the founder of Scientology: "However Hubbard may appear to his devoted followers, the Board can form no other view than that Hubbard is a fraud and Scientology fraudulent."

And in another place: "His sanity is to be gravely doubted."

In prompt reaction to the Report, Victorian Premier Sir Henry Bolte called a press conference to announce that the Government was duty bound to act on the Board's recommendations.

And so it did. In less than two months, the Victorian legislature passed what was called the Psychological Practices Act, 1965, whose principal aim was the banning of Scientology. In fact, it was at first known informally as the Scientology Prohibition Bill.

The chief provisions of the Act are:

It sets up a Psychological Council and requires the registration of psychologists with the Council; and restricts the practice of that profession for fee or reward, as well as the use of the word "psychologist", or similar expressions.

It imposes a fine of A$500 for use of the E-meter by anyone other than registered psychologists.

It makes it a criminal offence, punishable by a fine of $200 for the first conviction and up to two years' imprisonment for a second, to demand or receive directly or indirectly, any fee or reward for the teaching, practice or application of Scientology. The same restriction applies to holding oneself out as being willing to teach Scientology.

It directs all persons holding "Scientology records" to deliver them up to the Attorney-General and authorizes the seizure of such records by law enforcement officials.

Acting swiftly under terms of the last mentioned clause, within one half hour after passage of the bill, police raided the Scientology headquarters in Melbourne, where they confiscated some 4,000 documents, personal files and books.

The Scientologists' response to this draconian suppression in Victoria was to publish a booklet entitled *Kangaroo Court*, which laid bare the conspiracy and bias behind the Melbourne Inquiry and vowed that Scientology would continue to grow in Victoria. "No vested interests or blackhearted politicians, no matter how much power they seem to ally themselves with, can stop our thoughts or our communications ... Our administrative form could be altered, but not the subject of Scientology ... We will be here teaching and listening when our opponents' names are merely mis-spelled references in a history book of tyranny."

Later, Hubbard and his followers took more direct action. On April 28, 1970, a writ issued in the Supreme Court of the State of Victoria by the Hubbard Association of Scientologists International against Anderson and Just, charging the two with misfeasance, breach of duty and recklessness in the conduct of the Inquiry into Scientology.

This legal counter-attack created a considerable stir in Victorian professional and political circles. Following the Inquiry, both men had been elevated to judgeships – Anderson was now a Justice of the Supreme Court, and Just a judge of the County Court.

In order to block the Scientologists from having their case heard in a real court of law, where rules of evidence must be observed, Supreme Court Justice McInerny set aside the writ on a technicality. He ruled that Ian Tampion, acting as agent for the Scientologists, was "an unqualified person".

The Scientologists refused to give up. After considerable difficulty, they eventually found a firm of solicitors that would, acting as "qualified persons", properly lodge the writ in the Supreme Court.

Hubbard's organization now went even further and had writs issued not only against Anderson and Just, but against the Victorian Government (for libel in publishing the Anderson Report) and six newspapers.

This time the writs could not be struck out on the basis of some legal technicality. The defendants would have to face a full court hearing of the charges against them.

Then, in what was plainly a frantic last-ditch manoeuvre, the Victorian legislature took the unprecedented action of passing a *retroactive* law that conferred absolute immunity upon Anderson and Just. Entitled *Evidence (Boards and Commissions) Bill*, it amended the evidence Act, 1958 "to overcome separate problems brought to the attention of the Government by the Chief Justice and by the Crown Solicitor". Section 21A of the measure provided that "persons constituting a Royal Commission or board of inquiry, together with legal practitioners and others appearing before the commission or board, and witnesses shall have and *be deemed always to have had* the same privileges and immunities in respect of acts, matters or things done in relation to or arising in or out of the inquiry or the report of the inquiry as if they were done in relation to or arose in or out of a Supreme Court action or a report of such action." (Emphasis added.)

The idea of a retroactive law, designed to circumvent an

action pending before a Supreme Court, would be rejected by the legislature of any civilized state where jurisprudence has any meaning. Even in Victoria, where apparently the race is to the swift and the battle to the strong, a few honorable members rose during the parliamentary debate to go on record as *deploring* the measure and criticizing the Government (along party lines) for making such an extreme action necessary. But, having deplored the bill, they then voted in favour of it.

What seemingly incensed the dissenters most was the fact that the Attorney-General had tried to pull the wool over their eyes. In his speech before the House, explaining the bill, he had said that the aim of the legislation was to amend the Evidence Act to provide immunity for persons appointed to conduct Royal Commissions or boards of inquiry; but he did not inform the members that it was also designed to stop a writ already before the court. Said the member for Albert Park:

"We should have been told that a writ which was destined to come before the Supreme Court will be stopped in mid-air, as it were, by an action of this Parliament.

"The passage of this Bill through Parliament will indicate to many people that justice – in the sense of a person being able to plead his case in court – will not even get off the ground."

One of the most outspoken critics of the Past-Present-Future bill was the Hon. J. W. Galbally, the man who had started the legislative steam-roller against Scientology in the first place. Galbally expressed the view that if the law were amended retrospectively to put Scientologists out of court, it would only "put a sword in the hands of these thoroughly unworthy people".

"I should like to see their actions tried in the court," Galbally continued, "because even as the law stands, I do not think they would have any sort of case. If they win, let the Government pay up. I believe this would be a small price to pay for the independence of justice."

Such was not the majority view of the honorable gentle-men. Whether the Scientologists won or lost in court was not the question. The real issue was whether to allow the full story of the Inquiry to be aired in public.

"As Parliament appointed him [Anderson] to this position," said the Hon. C. A. M. Hider, "surely Parliament is bound to protect him and to avoid having a judge embarrassed."

Protecting Anderson was more important than preserving the integrity of the law itself.

Although Scientology had been outlawed – temporarily at least – in the State of Victoria, it was still flourishing elsewhere in Australia.

The medico-psychiatric group, together with their political and press allies who were conducting the extermination campaign against Scientology, now directed their efforts towards securing a nationwide ban on the organization. Health Minister G. C. MacKinnon of Western Australia told newsmen in January 1967 that he would call for such a ban at the Health Ministers conference to be held in Perth in April of the year.

MacKinnon made no secret of his motives. Scientology, he said, was dangerous "to certain groups in the community". He then made it clear which groups he was referring to:

"This is an organization which particularly argues against the established mental health services."[9] (p. 19)

True to his pledge, MacKinnon had the subject of Scientology put on the agenda of the Conference of Health Ministers. However, he was unable to get an agreement from all the ministers present to push for joint Commonwealth-State legislation against the "cult". Those in whose States there were no Scientology centres felt that it was up to the individual States to deal with the problem when and if it arose.

At the same time, for publicity purposes, a resolution was

passed condemning "the harmful cult" and recommending that "a close watch should be maintained to prevent its spread".

Scientology was even made the whipping boy for crimes which came before the courts. For example, when a male nurse in Sydney appeared in Quarter Sessions, after pleading guilty of an offence against an eight-year-old boy, Dr. Emmanuel Fisher, a psychiatrist and member of the World Federation of Mental health, gave expert testimony in his defence. Dr. Fisher told the court that Scientology was 99 per cent responsible for the man's criminal behaviour. He had attended the cult's lectures.

Thereupon, showing tender concern for an aggressive, adult pederast who had sexually assaulted a child, the magistrate – a Judge Monahan – released the man on a £100 bond and said he hoped his name would not be published. It wasn't.

While on the stand, Dr. Fisher was permitted to discuss two other wholly irrelevant cases in which he said he had treated two young people who had been attending lectures on Scientology.[10]

In another case, also before the Sydney Sessions, a Judge Amsberg said, after receiving psychiatric reports on an estate agent he had sentenced for fraudulently converting trust funds: "It is clear that a good deal of your mental difficulty is due to your association with people who call themselves Scientologists. It seems like an evil cloud settles on a person."

Declaring that "he has my deepest sympathy", Judge Amsberg then signed an order to have the defendant removed to a mental asylum where he would "receive proper psychiatric treatment".

In response to pressure brought by the State Health Council and others associated with that body, in November 1968 a bill was introduced in the Parliament of Western Australia similar to the one earlier passed by the State of Victoria; prohibiting the practice and teaching of

Scientology. Voting on the measure divided along party lines, with the government's majority of three insuring passage of the Act. During a lengthy debate of the Bill, H. Graham, deputy leader of the Opposition promised that "when a Labour Government is elected – whenever that might be – high on the list of priorities will be the repeal of this rotten piece of legislation".

Scientologists pointed out that Dr. A. S. Ellis, chairman of the State's Mental Health Committee, and one of the chief instigators of the Western Australian legislation, had attended the founding meetings of the World Mental Health Organization in 1948 and had served under Dr. E. Cunningham Dax for nearly ten years.

Soon after the outlawing of Scientology in Western Australia, a similar Bill was introduced in the South Australian legislature. Again, voting divided along party lines, with the Opposition solidly against it. When the vote was tied, the deciding vote in favour of the Bill was cast by Tom Scott, Speaker of the House. Scott's personal physician was an outspoken critic of Scientology and a member of the South Australian Association for Mental Health, a local affiliate of the World Federation for Mental health.

Opposition leader D. A. Dunstan, who had previously investigated Scientology when he was Attorney-General, told members of the House: "I must say that after a few complaints made to me about Scientology in South Australia, we investigated this matter, following *the urging of the Victorian Chief Secretary*. I had it drawn to my attention that there were a number of prominent citizens of standing in South Australia who could not in any way be said to be mentally unstable or unsatisfactory citizens (they were the reverse, being prominent in community organizations), who were involved in Scientology and who claimed to have derived personal benefit from it."[11] (Emphasis added.)

In reviewing the hearings that resulted in the Anderson

Report and those which followed the same pattern in the States of Western and Southern Australia, I do not see how any unbiased observer can escape the conclusion that they were political window-dressing. In all of them the findings were preconceived and the evidence highly selective and often distorted to support the *a priori* assumption that Scientology is evil. Furthermore, the language of the Reports which issued from the Inquiries is clearly propagandist rather than judicial.

In New Zealand, it was a different story. There for the first – and perhaps the last time – the case against Scientology was weighed in honest balances by men for whom, apparently, the truth meant more than accommodation to a politically powerful elite.

This does not mean that the New Zealand Commission of Inquiry gave Scientology passing marks in all the subjects that came before them. On the contrary, much of their report is unfavourable to Scientology. But in reading through the summary of their findings, one gets the strong impression that they are based on careful examination and analysis, not upon prejudice and pre-commitment. The criticisms offered are pretty much those that any fair-minded, non-Scientologist would make on the basis of the evidence presented. The Commission does not quote the Anderson Report, the U.S. Food and Drug Administration, nor the "expert" opinions of psychiatrists and cow-college professors of psychology – all with an axe to grind.

Instead, they addressed themselves to an impartial scrutiny of the activities, methods, and practices of the Hubbard Scientology Organization *in New Zealand*. At the opening of the session in Auckland, the Commission chairman stated that the hearings would not in general "extend to or include any inquiry into the 'philosophy, teachings or beliefs' of Scientology".

No evidence was given *in camera*.

The move against Scientology in New Zealand was begun in the usual way: on June 28, 1968, a petitition bearing 716 signatures was presented to Parliament, asking that a Board of Inquiry be set up to investigate Scientology, and requesting legislative action. The petitition was referred to the Select Committee on Social Services, which, after hearing evidence, recommended that the Inquiry be held.

The Commission was set up by Order in Council on February 3, 1969. Sir Guy Richardson Powles, the New Zealand Ombudsman and E. V. Dumbleton, retired newspaper editor were members of the Commission, with G. S. Orr as assisting counsel.

The Commission sat for eight days, during which they heard twenty-seven witnesses, whose testimony filled 650 pages of transcript.

The Report of their conclusions and recommendations was submitted to the Governor-General of New Zealand on June 30, 1969.

Throughout the Inquiry, the Commission was mainly concerned (and I believe, justifiably so) with a number of practices which Scientology lumped together under the heading of Ethics.

Officially, Ethics is defined as "rationality towards the highest level of survival for the individual, the future race, the group and mankind, and the other dynamics taken collectively. Ethics are reason and the contemplation of optimum survival".

That all sounds innocuous enough. The rub came in the security system which Hubbard and his followers developed to insure "optimum survival".

The problem, apparently, was twofold. There was a question of the individual preclear's progress, if he came under the criticism or opposition of someone in his immediate environment who was hostile to Scientology. There was also the need to deal with persons within the organization itself, who wanted to use Scientology as a nucleus for their own personal brand of technology, altering the procedures to fit their new concepts.

Scientology minister Robert H. Thomas explained the background of the first problem to me in these words:

"It was discovered a long time ago – in the early 60s – that certain individuals did not respond properly to processing. They seemed not to make gains the way we expect people to do. It was discovered that they had connections to the outside, or certain kinds of problems, or difficulties in their personal lives, which had to be handled before they could give enough attention even to get into an auditing situation and derive any benefit.

"In such cases, we would issue an order to that person, saying do this or do that, or you will not be given any further auditing. We found that the person having problems was connected to people outside who were antagonistic to Scientology; were, in fact, trying to destroy Scientology. As long as the preclear was connected to or under the influence or domination of such people, they would not progress because the hostile people were a continuing source of enturbulation."

The outside troublemakers (who were more often than not, close relatives, parents, or marital partners) were known as Suppressive Persons. If a Scientologist remained in association with them he was declared to be a Potential Trouble Source (PTS).

The only effective solution to such a situation was deemed to be a formal act of "disconnection" by the PTS from the people in his life who were threatening Scientology. This took the form of a letter from the Scientologist to the Suppressive person or persons, notifying them that thereafter they would be allowed no contact with the writer. The wording and length of the letters varied but their residual import was the same. The New Zealand Commission of Inquiry quoted the following, from a Scientologist to her aunt. It is fairly typical:

"I am disconnecting from you from now on. If you try to ring me, I will not answer, I will not read any mail you send, and I refuse to have anything to do with you in any way whatsoever. All communication is cut completely."

While such abrupt and seemingly permanent ruptures in intimate human relationships were often followed by greater consternation on the part of the Suppressive Person in some cases the individual who had taken that final step stood to benefit from it.

For a husband or wife who had been under the thumb of his or her domineering mate; or for the forty-year-old man still tied to his mother's apron strings, disconnection could only be a joyous emancipation.

However, from a human and community-relations point of view, there are better ways of dealing with such situations, as Scientology itself eventually came to see.

Scientology's Ethics division also was charged with maintaining the strict internal discipline that Hubbard felt was necessary to ensure the "optimum survival" of a world-wide organization like Scientology. A corps of Ethics officers, who combined the duties of both an intelligence service and a tribunal which heard evidence and meted out punishment to offenders, was established in every Scientology centre.

At one point in the development of this security system, the inevitable dissensions, weaknesses, and threats of ego-driven reformers who wanted to "take over" Scientology and run it according to their personal views, resulted in practices that were called "harsh ethics".

Disconnection was only one of the remedies imposed. Ethics could, for example, mete out other penalties ranging in severity from personal humiliation for minor offences, to criminal charges for serious or "High Crimes" such as treason.

Scientologists who became what Hubbard called a "down statistics" – i.e., a drawback to the advancement of the org. – might be required to wear a dirty grey rag on their left arms. They could "be employed at any additional work" and were subject to day and night confinement to premises.

For such misdemeanours as carelessness or neglect which resulted in expense to the org. – the offender could be confined in or barred from the premises. He was obliged to wear a handcuff on his left wrist.

Another and, it seems to me, even less excusable practice was that of declaring an enemy Fair Game. Any person so designated (by an Ethics Order) could be deprived of property or injured by any means, fair or foul. He could be "tricked, sued, or lied to, or destroyed".

How far Scientologists went in applying the Fair Game rule during that period of the movement's history, I do not know. Many ugly rumours and second-hand accounts of physical assaults, slander and false legal charges against those labelled Suppressive Persons have been circulated by ex-Scientologists and by Hubbard's avowed enemies. In any case, such practices can only be viewed with abhorrence by decent people; and that, indeed, is the way the Scientologists themselves, including Hubbard, seem to regard them in retrospect.

Granted that Hubbard was faced with the major problem that has plagued every religion or organization based upon ritualistic procedures – that of preserving the integrity of its body of doctrine – it seems to me it could have been handled in a more *Scientological* way.

At the same time, I have little patience with those who severely criticize Scientology for the strict discipline it imposes upon its adherents and yet find nothing blame-worthy in, say, the Roman Catholic practice of excommunication, doctrine of infallibility and system of canonical law, with its own lawyers and court of first and last instance.

Bob Thomas, Scientology's soft-spoken apologist who appears to have a rational explanation for every facet of his Church's operation told me:

"Of course, as with any great religious movement, we get the problem of holding the organization together. You come in with the old story of the man who was walking with the Devil when they saw somebody on the path ahead of them bend over and pick up an object. The man asked the Devil what the fellow had found, and the Devil said: 'He's found Truth.' The Devil's companion then asked him: 'Why does it make you so happy that he's found Truth?' And the Devil said: 'Because I'm going to help him organize it.'

"You see, any perception of truth has to be organized, and with organization comes the imposition of human frailty. So we try to strike a balance, a golden mean, between truth and organization."

In the face of growing uneasiness about harsh Ethics within the movement, and mounting hostility outside, in 1968 Hubbard ordered a public opinion survey of the Church's current structure and practices. According to Scientology spokesmen, 318, 885 questionnaires were sent to all parts of the world.

As a result of the replies received, Hubbard issued a directive dated November 15, 1968, cancelling the practice of disconnection, security checking, and fair game, and the writing down or otherwise recording of any confessional materials.

Later, in a policy letter of March 7, 1969, a continuing ameliorating of Ethics procedures was indicated.

"We are going in the direction of mild ethics and involvement with the Society," Hubbard wrote. "After 19 years of attack by the minions of vested interest, psychiatric front groups, we developed a tightly disciplined organizational structure.

"I don't like to see my friends pushed around. We didn't know it at the time, but out difficulties and failures were the result of false reports put out by the small but rich and powerful, group of individuals who would deny man freedom.

"Now that we know ... we will never need a harsh spartan discipline for ourselves.

"It has become apparent that such duress is not necessary when one has a technology which sets man free."

It was partly on the basis of these policy reforms that the New Zealand Commission of Inquiry recommended that no legislative action be taken against Scientology.

In concluding their Report, the commissioners set down a word of warning and advice. "The commission feels that for the future Scientology should regard as indispensable certain rules of practice. These are:

1. No reintroduction of the practice of disconnection.
2. No issue of Suppressive Person or Declaration of Enemy orders by any member to any other member of a family.
3. No auditing or processing or training of anyone under the age of twenty-one without the specific written consent of both parents; such consent to include approval of the fees (which shall be specified) to be charged for the course or courses to which the consent is applicable.
4. A reduction to reasonable dimensions of 'promotion' literature sent through the post to individuals, and prompt discontinuance of it when this is requested."

If the Scientologists in New Zealand would observe these rules, the Report added, "no further occasion for Government or public alarm should arise . . .".

Neither Hubbard nor his followers made any objection to these reasonable strictures, and the Church has continued to function in New Zealand without further interference by Government authorities.

"New Zealand," a leading English Scientologist told me, "is the only place where we have had a decent and favourable inquiry, and it is the only place where there is no member association of the World Federation for Mental Health."

When Australia's first Labour government in twenty-

174 / The Hidden Story of Scientology

three years took the reins in late 1972, the tide against Scientology began to turn. True to his party's promise that if Labour won in the December federal elections, Scientology ministers would be registered under the Australia Commonwealth Marriages Act, the new Attorney-General registered the Church a few months after taking office.

Australian law provides that such registration is all that is needed to establish religious bona fides throughout the country. It had the effect of anulling the anti-Scientology measure passed by the Victorian Parliament, West Australia's promise to repeal was honoured in 1973, and will undoubtedly speed action on a bill to repeal similar legislation in South Australia, still pending at this writing.

REFERENCE NOTES

1. Melbourne *Truth*, August 7, 1971.
2. Affidavit of Phillip B. Wearne, sworn to at Sydney, N.S.W., on February 12, 1969.
3. Melbourne *Truth*, May 30, 1964.
4. Melbourne *Herald*, May 26, 1964.
5. Melbourne *Truth*, June 15, 1964.
6. *The Sun*, June 17, 1964.
7. *The Age*, June 30, 1964.
8. Melbourne *Herald*, May 26, 1964.
9. *Daily News*, January 18, 1967.
10. *The Sun*, November 13, 1965.
11. Sydney *Morning Herald*, January 29, 1966.

8. *The IRS Role*

The power and political influence of Scientology's enemies had dealt the movement a crippling blow in Australia. There was no doubt about that. But it was still going strong in the United States, the country in which the annihilation campaign had begun.

The point of focus shifted once more to America. There, the ongoing efforts of the federal Food and Drug Administration had so far produced only limited results; and the ruling by a U.S. Appellate Court that Scientology was a bona fide religion dimmed the legal prospects as the case moved towards the Supreme Court.

There was one agency of the Government, however, whose vast, complex and ever-changing code of laws and regulations made it virtually impossible for a citizen or organization ever to win a final victory against it. That was the Internal Revenue Service.

Absolutism and tyranny are deeply ingrained in all bureaucracies; but the IRS these evils have been endowed with almost limitless power. No one is beyond its reach. That is why income tax laws had been used to put gangsters behind bars when the police failed in their job of digging up the evidence needed to convict them for their real crimes.

To the short-sighted, politically naive reader who asks what difference it makes that such means were used to "nail" a mobster, so long as he was put away, I have this to say:

As all history proves, such illegal methods of entrapment are first used against suspected criminals or unpopular victims; then are more widely applied to political figures and to individuals who challenge the regime or hold nonconformist views. Finally, all pretence of expediency gives way to unbridled despotism: they become the instruments of general coercion and personal revenge.

A judge of the U.S. District Court not long ago observed from the bench: "No sophisticated person is unaware that even in this very Commonwealth [Massachusetts] the Internal Revenue Service has been in possession of facts with respect to public officials which it has presented in order to serve what can only be called political ends, be they high or low. And the judge who knows the score is aware that every time his decision offends the Internal Revenue Service, he is inviting a close inspection of his own returns."[1] (pp. 258-9)

In a previous work I have examined in detail the odious techniques employed by the IRS intelligence division, and I will not discuss them at length here. Suffice it to say that there is documented evidence which shows that under the guise of ferreting out tax dodgers and racketeers, secret agents of the Internal Revenue Service have, with impunity and contempt, violated both State and Federal laws. Their criminal activities have included illegal wire-tapping; use of electronic snooping gear to spy upon innocent and guilty alike; interception and opening of sealed, first-class mail; breaking and entering private homes, offices and automobiles, without a search warrant, harassment of defence attorneys; and using bugged conference rooms in IRS offices, equipped with secret microphones and one-way mirrors to monitor privileged conversations between taxpayers and their legal counsellors or accountants.

After months of careful investigation of IRS practices by the Judiciary Subcommittee of the U.S. Senate, the committee chairman declared: "There appears to be a festering infection in the IRS."

Far from instituting the reforms that were urgently called for by the hearings, IRS officials secretly aided *Life* magazine in a political assassination of the Senator who had dared publicly to challenge their Gestapo-like tactics.

Scientologists have reason to believe that in the continuing and intensive investigation of their Church, IRS agents are employing some of the spying techniques described above.

The importance the Scientology surveillance programme has for the IRS is indicated by the fact that on September 2, 1970, S. B. Wolfe, director of the Audit Division, issued a lengthy three-page confidential supplement (42G(11)6G–53) to their Manual, describing the background of the Church and instructing district offices to be alert to identify any Scientology-type organizations filing returns.

A special, Scientology Case Report form (M–0696) was printed by the agency's National Office and distributed to each region's Exempt Organization Program Director.

In keeping with the IRS practice of disposing of investigational notes or information that might be subpoenaed in a court trial, the directive said: "On completion of this program, remaining stock of forms M–0696 should be destroyed. This report is exempt from control under IRM 1(20)16.35 (1)(f)."

When the Founding Church of Scientology first applied to the Internal Revenue Service in 1956 for exemption from Federal income taxes, the IRS granted the application owing to the fact that the Church was duly incorporated as a religious and educational organization in the District of Columbia.

Two years later, the federal tax agency sent the Church a letter withdrawing their tax-exempt status on the ground that the exposition and propagation of "tenets set forth in the books of L. Ron Hubbard, and related instruments of instruction relative to 'Scientology' in training courses, clinical courses and otherwise" did not constitute an exclusively religious or educational activity.

In other words, the IRS mandarins had arrogated to themselves the power which the federal judge previously quoted said "no official, high or petty" could exercise under our Constitution ... They had purported to determine what was and was not a religious belief.

To any but the most innocent it must be obvious that the initiative for the IRS action did not originate within the agency itself. The decision to revoke tax exemption after it had been granted was prompted by influences at work elsewhere.

We have already examined compelling evidence that such influences were indeed active behind the scenes. As an added example:

Six months before Scientology's trial in the U.S. Court of Claims, the director of AMA's Bureau of Investigation wrote a letter to David W. Meister, executive secretary of the Peoria Medical Society, in which he said: "For your confidential information, some agents of the Internal Revenue Service were in the office not too long ago and we gave them a bundle of information on 'Scientology', Hubbard and their operations."

Scientology attorneys filed a protest against the IRS ruling and asked reinstatement of their exempt status, but IRS refused.

The Church's response was to bring suit in the U.S. Court of Claims, arguing that the action taken by IRS was "arbitrary, prejudicial and erroneous".

The Internal Revenue Service answered by denying the charges and at the same time filing a counter-claim against the Founding Church for $3,262.75, together with interest, for the fiscal year beginning July 25, 1955 and ending June 30, 1956.

The trial did not begin until July 5, 1967. After six days of testimony by witnesses for both sides, the court ruled that the Church was not entitled to an exemption because part of its earnings inured to the benefit of private individuals.

According to the Government's own audit, Hubbard's entire income from all Scientology sources during the taxable years in issue (June 1955 through June 1959) averaged less than $20,000 a year, including royalty on his books and fees for lectures given by him at various Scientology congresses. Mrs. Hubbard, an officer of the Church, received an average of less than $4,000 per year, as did L. Ron Hubbard, Jr., who held responsible jobs in the organization.

In what Church attorneys called "argument by innuendo", the Government implied to the Court that the Hubbards were receiving immense sums of money from all Scientology Churches collectively and that on that basis the exemption ought to be denied the Founding Church of Scientology.

If this were true, asked Scientology lawyers, why hadn't the Government introduced evidence to that effect? The record was barren of any such evidence.

The Founding Church of Scientology immediately filed a petition for amendment of judgment or for a rehearing. A year later, the case was heard before the full court of seven judges.

The court carefully avoided the underlying issue of the case, that is, the question of whether the Government and the courts are entitled to judge or characterize a religious practice for purposes of allowing or denying tax exemption.

Writing the opinion for the court, Judge Collins declared: "The court finds it unnecessary to decide whether plaintiff is a religious or educational organization as alleged, since, regardless of its character, plaintiff has not met the statutory conditions for exemption from income taxation."

Thereafter, none of the precedent cases cited by the opinion were concerned with religious bodies. Instead, they involved such organizations as The Broadway Theatre League of Lynchburg, Va., Birmingham Business College, Texas Trade School and Underwriters' Laboratories, Inc.

The nit-picking, letter-of-the-law opinion cited as evidence that some of the Church's net earnings inured to the benefit of private individuals, included such bagatelles as the fact that Hubbard had use of an automobile at the organization's expense and that the Church provided and maintained a personal residence for Hubbard and his family. Mrs. Hubbard had received rent for property owned by her that was leased to the Church. And there was "a completely unexplained figure of $250, and loans of $800 were received in 1958–59". There was also the weighty fact that L. Ron Hubbard, Jr. had been reimbursed for expenditures of approximately $200 in 1957–8 and 1958–9. And so on.

The court concluded as a matter of law that the Founding Church of Scientology was not entitled to a tax-exempt status, and dismissed their petition.

If this ruling were allowed to stand, it would provide legal authority for the Internal Revenue Service to act against not only the Founding Church in Washington, but all the branch Scientology centres throughout the United States. The enormous sums in back taxes and interest that could be assessed for all the years involved could be ruinous to the Scientology movement in America.

The only remaining legal recourse open to the Founding Church of Scientology was to petition the Supreme Court to review its case. Accordingly, attorneys for the Mother Church asked the High Court for a writ of certiorari, arguing that denial of tax exemption to a particular religion constitutes discrimination among religions and is therefore a violation of the establishment clause of the First Amendment.

In opposition, government attorneys again dwelt upon the fees, royalties and compensation for services Hubbard had received and arrogantly asserted that, as "tax exemption is a matter of legislative grace, petitioner has the burden of clearly establishing a right to it".

The Supreme Court denied a writ of certiorari.

In my opinion, the fundamental issue inherent in the case was never argued – namely the question of whether a federal agency has the right to determine *any* of the financial matters of a Church.

The many thousands of followers of Scientology, with a few exceptions, seem to have derived more personal benefit and spiritual help for the money they spent than the parishoners of large, established Churches, whose vast wealth is today often expended in non-religious (and sometimes anti-religious) political undertakings.

The Government's rank hypocrisy, as well as the discriminatory practices involved in the whole question of tax exemption is nowhere more apparent than in the case of huge, tax-exempt foundations which have been permitted to donate countless millions of dollars to revolutionary groups whose avowed aim was the subversion and violent overthrow of American civilization.

As far back as 1953 Congress set up a special committee under the chairmanship of Rep. B. Carroll Reece to investigate the structure and operations of these giant tax-free organizations. But the shocking disclosures of the foundation-financing of the radical left were never given much play in the mass media. In his book, *Tragedy and Hope: A History of the World In Our Time*, Prof. Carroll Quigley tells why:

"It soon became clear," he wrote, "that people of immense wealth would be unhappy if the investigation went too far, and that the 'most respected' newspapers in the country, closely allied with these men of wealth, would not get excited enough about any of the revelations to make the publicity worth while, in terms of votes or campaign contributions."

Typical of the *quiet* way the masscom handles news of these tax-exempt corporations' immense contributions to the destructive elements in society was the "play" given the announcement of the left-handed Ford Foundation that it was giving $500,000 to the militant black racist organization, CORE. The press buried the story beneath wooden heads, far back in their newspapers among the indigestion pills and girdle adds. On TV screens, it was an almost subliminal one-liner.

Had even a fraction of the same sum been handed over to, say, the John Birch Society, there would have been screaming banners from New York to Honolulu.

The Ford Foundation has donated millions of dollars to other subversive and Communist-staffed organizations with only whispered accounts of their activities in the media.

The same is true of other foundations controlled by rich industrial families and international financial coteries.

The Internal Revenue Service has never seen fit, however, to question the use by these powerful foundations of enormous tax-free sums to subsidize violent revolution, despite the pious words of the Government attorneys when they told the court in the Scientology case:

"The exemption from tax is made in recognition of the benefit which the public derives from the activities of religious, charitable and educational organizations ... It is based on the theory that 'the Government is compensated for the loss of revenue by its relief from financial burden which would otherwise have to be met by appropriations from public funds, and by the benefits resulting from the promotion of the general welfare'."

It is hard to imagine what benefits the American public could derive from the race riots, campus unrest, Communist intrigues, left-wing political manoeuvres, and educational subversion which lavish grants from some of the big, tax-exempt foundations have promoted.

REFERENCE NOTE

1. Hearings, Senate subcommittee on administrative practice and procedure (Invasions of Privacy) 1965.

9. England: The Scramble for Stones

It has long been the boast of the British that England is the Mother of Parliaments; and, indeed, they have good cause for pride.

Yet, one wonders why, in 700 years, so little has been done to place the sacred power of Parliament beyond the reach of selfish politicians and autocratic Ministers, who often enlist it in the service of influential vested interests.

We have witnessed a particularly flagrant example of such subversion in the Victorian Parliament's action to defeat the ends of justice by passing a retroactive law that would block the fair hearing of a case pending in the High Court.

Far from censuring their opposite numbers in Australia, the honourable members in England cited the Melbourne inquisition as proof that Scientology was a social menace, requiring similar harsh measures in the United Kingdom.

The attack on Scientology in Britain did not reach the House of Commons until February 7, 1966, when Lord Balniel, MP, chairman of the National Association for

Mental Health, put down a question in which he asked Kenneth Robinson, the then Minister of Health: "In view of the scathing criticism by an official board of enquiry in Australia into the so-called practice of Scientology, surely the Rt. Hon. Gentleman considers it is in the public interest to hold a similar type of enquiry in this country?"

The Rt. Hon. Gentleman (himself a former officer of the NAMH) replied that he was prepared "to consider any demand for an enquiry", but that no such demand had been made prior to that time.

"I am aware," he added, "that extravagant claims are made on behalf of Scientology, which are not generally accepted, and for my part, I would advise anyone who is considering a course of this kind to go to his doctor first."

This brief exchange was a curtain-raiser for the Parliamentary performance that was to follow – a performance carefully stage-managed by directors of the mental health movement and based upon the Melbourne scenario, which they regarded as a masterwork. They had pounced upon the Anderson Report with the delight of a burglar who finds a window open.

Health Minister Robinson was well-suited to his role both by birth and by experience. His father had been a doctor and his mother a nurse. Prior to assuming his Ministerial responsibilities, he had been prominently active in NAMH affairs, chairing various committees and serving as the association's vice-president.

In 1960, Robinson had made an extensive, NAMH-sponsored study-tour of mental institutions in Holland, France, the United States and Russia.

The Travelling Fellowship which provided for the expenses Robinson incurred on his trip and paid him a fee of £752 for handling the assignment, merits a brief examination.

On June 16, 1960, a New York law firm wrote William T. Beatty II, president of the World Federation for Mental Health, stating that they represented the Bruern

Foundation, which was desirious of making a contribution of £2,000 to the NAMH in England "for its general purposes".

"It had been suggested," the letter continued, "that this contribution might be made through your organization. The thought was that either you might remit the sum directly to the English organization or by making funds available to it in this country accomplish the same result."

The letter was not entrusted to the mails, but was delivered to the WFMH offices by messenger.

But why all the hugger-mugger? If the Bruern Foundation wanted to contribute £2,000 to the English mental health group, why was it necessary to funnel the money in CIA fashion through another organization?

Perhaps a partial answer to that question may be found in the identity and tax-status of the Bruern Foundation itself. At the time of the donation, the Foundation had applied to the U.S. Internal Revenue Service for tax exemption but had not received it. Subsequent investigation revealed that the Foundation (which has never, so far as I can determine, been listed in any directory of American foundations) was established by a member of the Astor family who was a British subject with business assets in the U.S.

The task of effecting transfer of the £2,000 was referred to Jonathan Bingham, counsel for the WFMH, who in turn passed it on to J. R. Rees, the world organization's director in Great Britain. Dr. Rees arranged for the money to be sent to Mary Applebey, general secretary of the National Association for Mental Health, in London.

The lurid charges against Scientology contained in the Anderson Report were not, in themselves, sufficient to raise the wind in England.

While the report provided provocative copy for the press (it was referred to in the British media 278 times in the space of five months), it would be necessary to discover tracks of the cloven hoof nearer home to produce the proper *frisson* among the Honourable Members.

In the latter part of August 1966, the *Daily Mail* made straight the way for certain MPs once again to raise the question of an inquiry into Scientology.

The newspaper published a lengthy article under the heading *The Case of the Processed Woman*, concerning a young woman who had been compulsorily detained in a mental ward after having been associated with Scientologists at Saint Hill Manor in East Grinstead.

The thirty-year-old woman had been in and out of mental hospitals (those "nurseries of insanity", as John Reid called them), since she was nineteen. It can therefore be assumed that psychiatric treatments had done for her before she ever met the Australian Scientologist who, on his own initiative, introduced her to Scientology. Nevertheless, the published account placed the blame for her mental breakdown upon Scientology processing.

The story was not, as the *Daily Mail* held out, the result of a thoroughgoing probe into the affair by its nose-to-the-trail investigative reporters. It was, rather, based upon information made available to the paper by the patient's mother (a certified Communist), who was willing to expose the personal details of her helpless daughter's condition in the public prints in order to "get" Scientology.

In a face-saving note at the end of the account, the newspaper declared: "The *Daily Mail* publishes the patient's name with the support and approval of her family who feel that the practices of Scientology should be made fully public."

Mary Applebey, general secretary of the National Association for Mental Health, was quoted in the Processed Woman story as saying, "Now the time has come when there should be a Ministerial inquiry."

It was like pressing the button to release jack-in-the-box. Up popped Peter Hordern, Conservative member from Horsham, to demand that the Health Minister, Kenneth

Robinson, initiate "an inquiry into the practice known as Scientology".

In a written answer, the minister said he did not think any further inquiry was necessary to establish that the activities of that organization were potentially harmful.

Actually, there was not yet enough "evidence" to sustain even a loaded-dice inquiry such as that staged in Melbourne. Accordingly, no move was made to set up formal hearings. Instead, Robinson limited his attack to a public denunciation, apparently hoping that the mental-health Amalekites would leave it at that.

A few months later, however, the Hon. Mr. Hordern took the floor just before midnight to make Scientology the subject of the motion for adjournment. He recalled that he had asked the Minister of Health on December 5 last to hold an inquiry into Scientology.

At that time, he went on, the Minister's reply was quite unsatisfactory because "it completely ignored the considerable body of evidence that had been laid before him by myself and others, and the great weight of evidence produced by the State of Victoria Commission, upon the evil nature of this organization".

Hordern, then, "with the express permission of her mother", recounted in detail once more the story of the "processed woman". He followed that dramatic account with a lengthy recital of findings from the Anderson Report, and ended with yet another appeal for a full inquiry into Scientology at the earliest possible date.

Mr. Geoffrey Johnson Smith (Conservative, East Grinstead) assured the House members that he had received information (source and kind not disclosed) "which would indicate that the case which we heard from my Hon. Friend the Member from Horsham, is not an isolated example, information which would add substance to the arguments which have been put forward".

Health Minister Kenneth Robinson still did not feel enough solid ground under his feet to proceed with a full-dress inquiry. Once again deploring Scientologists who "direct themselves deliberately towards the weak, the unbalanced, the immature, the rootless and mentally or emotionally unstable", the Minister said he was nevertheless still opposed to an inquiry. He added: "I have not had evidence that Scientology has been directly and exclusively responsible for mental breakdown or physical deterioration in its adherents in this country. I nevertheless intend to go on watching the position."

If more evidence were needed, Scientology's adversaries were resolved, in one way or another, to supply it. A brief article in the spring 1968 edition of *Mental Health* informed that publication's readers that "the chief, long-standing opponent of Scientology, Mr. Peter Hordern, Conservative MP for Horsham, is beginning to agitate for a public enquiry again. He has received many letters from disenchanted members – many too frightened to put a signature to what they write."

These poison-pen missives, including the many anonymous ones, were duly passed along to the Minister of Health to become part of what the Hon. Gentleman later described as "a considerable body of evidence about the activities of the cult in this country", but which he never exposed to public scrutiny.

The continuing pressure built up at the Ministries of Health, of Education and Science, and at the Home Office, eventually resulted in administrative action against the Scientologists. On July 25, 1968, in response to Mr. Johnson Smith's question in the House as to what action he proposed to take concerning Scientology, Kenneth Robinson replied:

"The Government are satisfied, having received all the available evidence, that Scientology is socially harmful. It alienates members of families from each other and attributes squalid and disgraceful motives to all who oppose it; its authoritarian principles and practice are a potential menace to the personality and well-being of those so deluded as to become its followers; above all, its methods can be a serious danger to the health of those who submit to them. There is evidence that children are now being indoctrinated.

"There is no power under existing law to prohibit the practice of Scientology; but the Government have concluded that it is so objectionable that it would be right to take all steps within their power to curb its growth.

"It appears that Scientology has drawn its adherents largely from overseas, though the organisation is now making intensive efforts to recruit residents of this country. Foreign nationals come here to study Scientology and to work at the so-called College in East Grinstead. The Government can prevent this under existing law (the Aliens Order), and have decided to do so. The following steps are being taken with immediate effect:

(a) The Hubbard College of Scientology, and all other Scientology establishments, will no longer be accepted as educational establishments for the purpose of Home Office policy on the admission and subsequent control of foreign nationals;

(b) Foreign nationals arriving at United Kingdom ports who intend to proceed to Scientology establishments will no longer be eligible for admission as students;

(c) Foreign nationals who are already in the United Kingdom, for example, as visitors, will not be granted student status for the purpose of attending a Scientology establishment;

(d) Foreign nationals already in the United Kingdom for study at a Scientology establishment will not be granted extensions of stay to continue those studies;

(e) Work permits and employment vouchers will not be issued to foreign nationals (or Commonwealth citizens) for work at a Scientology establishment;

(f) Work permits already issued to foreign nationals for work at a Scientology establishment will not be extended."

This announcement was made at the final session of Parliament before adjournment for holidays. It thus precluded any adequate deliberation or debate by the members on the issue. Furthermore, sufficient hard evidence to support such a drastic measure had not been presented.

It was all shamelessly unfair, and the more responsible elements of the British press began to smell a rat. These knights of the ballpoint lance did not care what happened to Scientologists (indeed, it was largely with their assistance that the situation was what it was), but they suddenly came to their senses long enough to realize that the arrogant and arbitrary exercise of power by Government administrators threatened not only the freedom of Scientologists, but their own as well.

"The Aliens Order," declared the *Sunday Times*, "under which all identifiable Scientologists have been denied entry to Britain places enormous power in the hands of the Home Secretary ... The case against Scientology does not yet seem monumental enough to justify this kind of treatment. As we show on another page, there is considerable doubt about how many complaints against the movement, on serious clinical grounds, have in fact been made."

The *Manchester Guardian* noted that they were "watching with discomfort the witch-hunt launched against the Scientologists". Rhetorically, they asked: "Since when has the Minister of Health been custodian of the authenticity of philosophies? This is government out of 'Erewhon.' ... Such ministerial decisions as this should be questioned all the way. The future of more than Scientology is involved in them."

Writing in the London *Daily Express*, columnist Robert Pitman observed that only the previous summer, the Minister of Health had said that health charges would be against all social progress. "A few months later, he was introducing them personally. Did he have a revelation, perhaps? As he was walking the Road to Whitehall, did the clouds open and a flat Northern voice declare: 'Kenneth, Kenneth, why kickest thou against the charges?' "

The lush outpourings of anti-Scientology stories which had appeared in the media were now re-examined in a more sober light and found to be largely back-fence gossip.

"Rummaging through a bewildering heap of new press clippings about the Church of Scientology," wrote C. H. Rolph in the *New Statesman*, "I find that the recent fuss began with a *Daily Mail* 'Newsight' article and that since then, with two exceptions, all the pressmen have been quoting each other."

Why, asked Rolph, did Scientology have to be suddenly proscribed as something socially harmful in a way that other cults were not, "its practitioners and pupils deported, its children barred from schools, its members turned down by motor and accident-insurance companies, even its meetings outlawed? Once you start this sort of thing, everyone scrambles for stones."

Another manifestation of the uneasiness felt by the more alert segments of British society concerning the rule by administrative fiat as demonstrated in the Scientology ban, was the action taken by the National Council for Civil Liberties. Describing Robinson's statement on Scientology in Commons as "particularly fatuous", the Council's chairman, Tony Smythe, said: "Mr. Robinson's remarks would apply with more justification to the Catholic Church, and if he objected to the Pope's views, he could presumably harass Catholics in the same way."

Smythe added that the Council considered such administrative measures as the ban against Scientologists to be totally wrong and would fight it.

When Commons reconvened in the autumn, voices of dissent were also raised in that august chamber. Some of the unmortgaged Members on both sides of the House challenged the Health Minister to publish the evidence he claimed to have in his possession and upon which he based his statements and actions against Scientology.

Mr. Robinson could not, of course, produce something which quite obviously he did not have. He took cover behind the shield so widely used by government functionaries in all countries – the alleged confidentiality of his information. Detailed evidence proving the cult's potential danger to health, said he, consisted of individual case histories which it would be inappropriate to make public.

Referring to the massive attack in the media, Robinson declared with a straight face that evidence of Scientology's social dangers had already been published widely in the press.

Enforcement of the ban on foreign Scientologists soon led British authorities into actions that were sometimes cruel and at other times ludicrous. Immigration officials were charged, as Conservative MP Iain Macleod observed, with the absurd task of trying to divide mankind into Scientologists and the rest.

It was not practical, of course, to ask every alien visitor arriving in England whether he was a Scientologist (although such a procedure would have greatly pleased the Scientologists; it's the kind of publicity you can't buy).

The Cerberean guards at the gates of Albion had to depend upon tips from Hubbard-haters, official reports, customs agents (who reported Scientology literature in the traveller's luggage), and the answer to a question appearing on the Landing Card as to the foreigner's reason for coming to Britain.

There were also less reputable sources of information. Scientologists at Saint Hill Manor are certain that their mail was intercepted and their telex and telephones tapped.

Since even the most sophisticated electronic equipment will not detect a wire tap that is made by officials who have the co-operation of the telephone company, the staff at Saint Hill tested the privacy of their lines in a simpler, but far more effective way.

At a certain time, a call was made from the East Grinstead headquarters to a branch centre. The person receiving the call was informed (falsely) that L. Ron Hubbard was entering England in defiance of the ban. He would arrive at a given airport at a given time.

Scientologists waited at the airport to meet not Mr. Hubbard, but representatives of the Home Office. They were not disappointed. Shortly before the time Mr. Hubbard was supposed to arrive, a corps of Home Office minions showed up in official cars and deployed around the area reserved for processing incoming passengers.

The splendid turnout of officials to receive the non-arriving L. Ron Hubbard was cogent proof that the telephones at Saint Hill were well-monitored.

While individual Scientologists who came to Britain found little difficulty in passing through the permeable immigration barrier set up to keep them out, those who travelled in groups were prevented from entering.

In July 1968, for example, a charter flight which was to bring 186 American students to Scotland was cancelled by the airline after being informed by the Home Office that the Scientologists would not be allowed to enter the United Kingdom.

Less than one month later, 200 South Africans and 600 Americans, who wanted to attend a Scientology congress in London, were refused admission.

At the entrances to the Croydon hall where the congress was held, squads of Scotland Yard detectives screened delegates entering the building.

Home Office commissars issued a warning to foreign visitors that anyone who came to Britain to attend the Scientology conclave, but put down "holiday" on his landing card, as the purpose of his visit, would be guilty of an offence.

In an action that must have surprised and greatly annoyed the Yanks who were not Scientologists, immigration officers asked every American arriving in Britain

13—HSOS • •

during the period just preceding the congress: "Why have you come here?"

Thoughtful Britons began to view this wholesale and almost hysterical zenophobia with growing concern. It publicly called into question the traditional and widely-held belief that the British were somehow more enlightened and tolerant in their views than the people of less civilized countries.

Mr. Alexander Lyon, Labour MP for York, asked the Home Secretary how many persons had been denied entry into the United Kingdom on the ground that they were Scientologists; and under what powers the immigration officers acted in refusing entry.

In his written reply, James Callaghan clearly demonstrated the fact that "credibility gap" is not a phenomenon confined to high-level government circles in Washington. He said:

"No one has been refused admission on the sole ground that he was a Scientologist; but since July 25, 104 foreign nationals intending to study at Scientology establishments have been refused leave to land, under the Aliens Order, 1953."

Although it was one of the stories that Fleet Street somehow overlooked, the harassment of overseas students coming to England to study Scientology began even *before* the Home Office officially announced its ban on foreign nationals.

By far the worst example of disregard for human rights or even human decency by Government gauleiters occurred in late June 1968. Two young new Zealanders – Sandra Stevens, eighteen and Bruce Gibson, twenty-four – who made the long journey from the antipodes to take a six-month course in Scientology at Saint Hill – were refused entry by the chief immigration officer at Heathrow Airport.

They were taken into custody and detained in prisons for

convicted criminals, while legal representations were being made on their behalf.

Sandra, who was sent to Holloway Prison for women, told her story in these words:

"The first time I realized there might be trouble ahead was on the plane. A man sitting beside me told me that, being a Scientologist, I would have trouble getting into England. I merely laughed and told him that we were talking about England, after all, and in England you were allowed to believe in what you chose. He laughed back at me and said – 'You'll see'. *I did!*

"On landing at London Airport and after passing quickly through Health I was stopped at Immigration and asked about my religion. Which level I was at and whether I had come to study in East Grinstead. I had all my luggage searched and my personal papers and letters taken away and read.

"After a two hour wait I was subjected to twenty minutes' questioning of my religion by two Immigration Officers. Only when I asked what my religion had to do with my being detained was I asked about the amount of money that I had and whether I had a return ticket. I showed them a letter saying I was being supported at £10 per week and told them any ticket would be paid at the end of my course.

"Another two hours went by. After that we were shunted into the office of the Chief Immigration Official. My travelling companion and I were told that we were going to be deported to Hong Kong that afternoon. An official told us that this action was being taken because I was a Scientologist.

"We rang the College at Saint Hill and managed to put off deportation to the following morning. One staff member from Saint Hill brought a letter saying we were students. I phoned home and asked them to cable 200 dollars and to organize return air fare – which was done. We also rang the N.Z. High Commissioner, only to be told that as N.Z.

citizens and members of the Commonwealth we had no rights.

"The following morning – still at the airport – Immigration changed our tickets. Since sufficient funds and return fare had been guaranteed, they now told us that we would be refused entry on grounds that we had no work permits and were 'Student Trainees'.

"The Legal Officer from Saint Hill came to the airport and took the legal battle off our hands.

"We had to stay at the airport, and then Bruce, my fellow-traveller and also a Scientology student, was transported to Brixton prison and I was taken to Holloway prison. This was the beginning of a new ordeal that was to last for nine days before I was allowed to leave the prison.

"When I arrived I was told to take off all my clothes, my belongings were taken from me and gone carefully through. I was left with one set of my own clothes and a prison nightdress. I was then taken up to my cell, which had no toilet or any facilities and a barred window.

"When the heavy door was shut and the key turned in the lock, I was very upset and felt all alone. There was a glaring light in my room and I couldn't sleep. I pressed what I thought was the light switch and a loud buzzer jangled through the corridors. The night guard rushed up and asked angrily what was wanted. I told her that I wanted the light off. The answer was that the lights were left on all night in the solitary wings. I was in solitary though I had committed no crime.

"I woke up at dawn and lay awake until 7 a.m. when we were all pulled out of bed. I went upstairs with my bucket to wash. I was just about to get dressed when a girl from another cell came in. 'Hi, I'm Gale. I'm a lesbian. Can I have a fag?' In a few minutes there were three of them surrounding me, asking me for cigarettes – they also stole some off me later.

"After an unspeakable 'breakfast' consisting of porridge without milk or sugar – not to speak of jam – and some old bread, we were taken upstairs to work. 'Work' consisted of pushing out beer mats from a large piece of cardboard and counting them into lots of 100.

"That morning I was called out to see a Presbyterian minister, but when I told him I was not from his Church, he shrugged his shoulders and said there was nothing he could do for me.

"I was then taken to have my chest X-rayed. I was also asked to have a VD test, but managed to have that order withdrawn after explaining some naïve facts of life.

"The girls in prison treated me with a certain respect and said I didn't belong with them in prison. They were there for murder, drugs and theft. I was told in precise details how lesbians are lesbians, about drugs, prostitution and larceny.

"We were allowed no visitors except legal, and relatives and letters out were limited to one a week, all censored, of course.

"Being a responsible person, I was given the 'privilege' of being a 'garden girl'. The job consisted of picking up a heavy barrow, filling it full with dirt and unloading at the other end of the road. Then run back for another load. After hours of work my hands were full of blisters and neck and shoulders ached.

"One night two girls smuggled in some 'hash' cigarettes and smoked them amongst themselves. One girl threw an epileptic fit. She fell on the floor, bit her tongue till blood streamed from her mouth. When she had calmed down a bit she was brought back to her solitary.

"One girl obviously didn't like my looks – she glared at me, then picked up a chair and threw it at me. Other girls tried to hold her down. She repeated this twice.

"I was allowed to leave prison after nine days. I had learned more about the sordid sides of life in those nine days than all my life before. I had read about prisons – I never thought it would become a reality for me."[1]

When the case was finally heard before a tribunal, the

High Court judge ordered her release and gave costs against the Home Office.

The petty harassments and ignoble acts that have always been a part of religious persecutions were not wanting in Scientology's British experience.

Members of the Church (and here I am referring to English members, not foreign nationals) were made the victims of various kinds of slander, discrimination and spite. Here are some typical instances:

The headmaster of a private school refused to accept the son of a prominent Scientologist as a pupil, declaring, "The father has drawn a great deal of attention to himself and the family belongs to an organization said to be socially harmful."

Six doctors in East Grinstead, Sussex (home of Scientology's world headquarters) refused to accept Scientologists as patients on their National Health Service lists. A spokesman for the group told newsmen that "ethical reasons" prevented his stating his objections. A lay member of the East Sussex National Health Executive Council made a public statement, saying:

"It is within my official knowledge that local doctors are most unwilling to include Scientologists in their lists of patients for the reason that they naturally want to avoid association with people who are frequently unclean and are often found living in most unsatisfactory conditions."⁵

Britains largest insurance company, the Royal Insurance Group, withdrew its policy on Scientology's international headquarters – Saint Hill Manor. The reason given by company executives was that "we are pruning our portfolio of unprofitable business".

When the Scientologists purchased an advertisement in the Tunbridge Wells telephone directory, it appeared under the classification, *Zoos*. Later the Government Post Office wrote to Thomson Directories, who print the book, asking them not to carry any more advertising for Scientology under any classification.

The ability of the group fighting Scientology to use even the Foreign Office to harass Hubbard and his followers in distant parts of the world (and I am convinced they did, despite official denials) should make even the most resolute flagwaver stop and think.

Consider, by way of illustration, the Corfu caper. Anyone who has read any of the many accounts of British war-time intelligence activities will immediately recognize a familiar pattern in the whole episode.

Hubbard and 200 of his adherents who had taken up residence aboard the 3,300-ton ship *Apollo*, thought they had found a haven far removed from their tormentors, when they docked in the harbour of Corfu, a Greek island in the Ionian Sea.

The local population was friendly, their goodwill no doubt stimulated by the estimated $50,000 a month the Scientologists were pouring into the island economy, which had to depend ordinarily on what summer tourism brought in.

After five or six halcyon months in their Greek refuge, however, the Scientologists began to realize that their enemies were at work once more behind the scenes, planting suspicions against Scientology in the minds of local authorities and spreading false stories among the people concerning the foreign "cult".

According to the Scientologists' account of the affair, a substantial part of which I later verified, the main focal point of their difficulties in Corfu was the Honorary British Vice-Consul, a certain Major John Forte, whom Hubbard followers suspected, rightly or wrongly, of making derogatory statements about them to the Greek authorities.

An article appeared in the Corfu newspaper, *Telegrafos*, warning the Scientologists that the Greek Government would not tolerate anyone spreading within her territory theories of religion, politics "or even of black magic".

Since all of Scientology's literature was in English and the people of Corfu spoke Greek, such a statement leaves one puzzled as to how Hubbard might proselytize the local population. It seemed, rather, a pretext for publishing the whispered gossip already being circulated by word of mouth.

In London, the Greek Embassy was given copies of *Hansard* which reported in full the adjournment debate of March 6, 1967 concerning Scientology, as well as the Health Ministers statement of policy to the House on July 25, 1968, when he announced the ban against foreign Scientologists.

Apparently to make certain that the information reached Greek Government authorities at home, the British Embassy in Athens made the same material available to the Greek Deputy Prime Minister there.

The American State Department also weighed in with a request to Greek authorities for information concerning a thirty-one-year-old woman from Las Vegas, whose parents said had been kidnapped by the Scientologists. The woman had been aboard the *Apollo*, but had left the ship some time previously. Hubbard was unable to inform the Greek officials of the woman's whereabouts because he did not know. Later, she turned up in Athens and expressed surprise that everybody had been searching for her. "We wonder," said a Scientology spokesman, "which Embassy or Embassy official hid her all that time."

In exasperation, the Greek government on March 18, 1969 ordered the Scientologists to leave Greece. In reporting the incident, the *New York Times* wrote: "The expulsion order followed months of diplomatic pressure in Athens by U.S., British and Australian diplomats urging Greek authorities to examine the activities of those aboard the *Apollo*."[2]

Not long afterwards, when the Greek authorities' own investigation revealed the truth concerning the Scientologists, Interior Minister Stylianos Pattakos apologized for the incident and invited Hubbard and his followers to return to Greece.

The British Foreign Office vigorously denied that Major Forte had had anything to do with the spreading of rumours about the *Apollo* and her crew. Nevertheless, a small item appearing in British papers on September 2, 1971 informed their readers that Major John Forte, Britain's representative for thirteen years on the Greek island of Corfu had been sacked and would be paid £1,000 compensation by the Foreign Office.

"The major blamed the sacking on his fight against the Scientology cult whose leader's 'flagship' spent nine months anchored off Corfu," said the story.[4] (p. 9)

Major Forte's dismissal came soon after Sir John Foster, who was conducting an official inquiry into Scientology, asked the Foreign Office to investigate the Corfu incident.

Hubbard charged that Major Forte was an agent acting under orders of the Foreign Office's "Black Propaganda" department. During the war, MI6, Britain's Secret Intelligence Service, actually operated such a branch whose function was to spread rumours and bits of gossip that would mislead and subvert the enemy, and "destroy them with whispers". The false stories were referred to as "sibs" among the secret agents, a word derived from the Latin *sibullare*, meaning "to whisper".

Scientologists pointed out that Christopher Mayhew, president of the National Association for Mental Health, had been one of the important figures in the wartime black propaganda section of MI6.

Furthermore, Richard Crossman, Secretary of State for the Social Services, who had succeeded Kenneth Robinson when the latter lost his portfolio, had also been one of the master minds in Britain's cloak-and-dagger operations during the war. A left-wing Socialist, he was at one time director of the German Section where, according to Sefton Delmer's memoirs in *Black Boomerang*, he took "a sort of

202 | The Hidden Story of Scientology

benevolent interest" in a group of German Marxists who helped in the psychological battle against Hitler.

Malcolm Muggeridge, who was himself connected with British intelligence, but who apparently had a low regard for its war-time personnel, who he described as a collection of "oddities, misfits and delinquents", said most of the agents were leftists who, in the various Resistance Movements with which they were associated, tended to favour the Communists.

"It is ironical," Muggeridge observed, "to recall now that the French and Italian Communists got the money and arms which enabled them to establish themselves so strongly after the war, not from Stalin, but from Anglo-American secret Intelligence sources."[3] (p. 184)

Scientologists say that even before the Corfu trouble, they had evidence that British agents were planting suspicions about them with foreign governments. They assert that one of their members who had a peek in the files of the Spanish Marine Ministry found reports from both the British Home and Foreign Offices, which implied that Scientology's floating contingent were smugglers under investigation by Interpol.

In Casablanca, a man who claimed to be a correspondent for the *Manchester Guardian* turned up at the Panamanian Consulate, stating that he was collecting information for a story on the Scientologists. (The *Apollo* was of Panamanian registry.)

Scientologists claim that the "newsman" informed the Panamanian Consul, as well as the local newspaper that they were drug traffickers wanted by Interpol for smuggling hashish into France and South America.

In their newspaper, *Freedom* (No. 27), the Scientologists announced (no doubt with tongue-in-cheek) that "to protect ourselves we are currently spreading the rumour that 'C' (which is what the head of MI6 is cutely called) has had a nervous breakdown and that MI6 is being run by C's psychiatrist, who studied twelve years to become an expert Communist. Two can play this game."

When Scientology was debated in the House of Commons on a motion for adjournment in March 1967, the Minister of Health had said that the Government took the view that there was little point in holding an enquiry because they already had evidence that the practice of Scientology was potentially harmful to its adherents.

The following year, when he announced the ban against foreign Scientologists, the Minister had repeated that assertion: "My Right Hon. Friend the Home Secretary and I have amassed a considerable body of evidence about the activities of the cult in this country."

Only seven months later, on January 27, 1969, Richard Crossman, Secretary of State for Social Services, informed the House of Commons that he was setting up an inquiry into Scientology.

To take executive action against the Church, as the Government had done, and then to establish an inquiry to determine whether official action was justified, recalled the Red Queen in *Alice in Wonderland*, who cried, "Sentence first – verdict afterwards."

Several of the Honourable Members wondered why.

"May I inquire," asked Mr. C. Pannell, "why it is that first, Scientology is characterised as a fraud, and then we set up an inquiry into it? Would it not have been rather better the other way round?"

Sir G. Nabarro was puzzled by the Government's sudden about-face: "May I now be told by the Hon. Gentleman what has caused him to relent and to change his mind, and why he is now doing exactly the opposite of what it was endeavoured to persuade him to do a few months ago?"

Mr. Crossman had no forthright answer to these queries, and in reply expressed bewilderment that they should be raised, then talked around and around the subject without saying anything.

To carry out the Inquiry, which had the broadest terms of reference, the Government named Sir John Foster, KBE, QC, MP, Conservative Member for Northwich.

Sir John's *curriculum vitae* followed the traditional pattern of England's ruling class. Educated at Eton and New College, Oxford, he became a barrister and later a Queen's Counsel. Prior to World War II, he lectured in international law at Oxford and afterwards became First Secretary at the British Embassy in Washington.

Crossman said the Inquiry would be conducted by Sir John alone, not by a committee and that it would not be carried out under statutory powers; therefore no one would be required to give evidence. Moreover, such evidence as was volunteered would be taken privately and not on oath.

"I have done this for a very special reason," explained Mr. Crossman. "The kind of evidence we want will be from people of a nervous nature, who will not face cross-examination or any public examination. This way we are more likely to get them to talk than in any other form of inquiry."

To Scientologist ears this sounded suspiciously like a secret tribunal before which lies, gossip and suspicion would be the only evidence to be heard. By excluding press and public and allowing Scientology's enemies to make charges unchallenged by cross-examination and unrestrained by swearing to tell the truth, the Government had set up an Inquisition along the lines followed by Torquemada.

Even unverified testimony from overseas countries was to be accepted.

The semi-privileged form the Inquiry was to take provoked adverse comment in several of Britain's leading newspapers, but it proceeded as scheduled.

Sir John Foster concluded his Inquiry on December 31, 1970, and submitted his written report a few months later. But Sir Keith Joseph, who had by that time succeeded

Richard Crossman as Minister for Social Services, showed a strange reluctance to publish it or to disclose its contents.

After months of "waiting for Sir Keith", both MPs and newspapers began to evince a growing impatience.

A *Daily Mail* reporter who had somehow learned what was in the Foster Report wrote that the Inquiry's findings had infuriated senior Government health experts, who had been behind the ban against Scientologists. He said the report could damage Whitehall reputations.

In Parliament, too, demands were heard for public disclosure of Sir John's conclusions, based on his examination of Scientology and its activities. During the three years since the ban had been imposed, some Members, on their own initiative, had taken steps to learn the facts about the sect and its practices.

William Hamling, Labour MP for Woolwich West, had gone personally to Saint Hill Manor and had taken several courses in Scientology. He said that he had found them very useful and thereafter became a supporter of the movement. The interesting thing about Mr. Hamling was that he had been Private Secretary to Health Minister Robinson who had taken steps to bar foreign adherents from entering Britain.

In response to public pressure, the Foster Report was finally published on December 22, 1971. One of its two principal conclusions, which had stunned the mandarins in Whitehall, was that most of the Government's measures against Scientologists were not justified and that the entry ban on foreign Scientologists entering Britain should be lifted.

The Report also criticized the roughshod way in which immigration officers had enforced the ban. They were, said Sir John, "even more stringent than the letter of the measures".

While it was clear that, as a matter of law, the Secretary of State for Home Affairs was perfectly within his rights in refusing Scientologists permission to enter Britain, "the mere fact that someone is a Scientologist is, in my opinion, no reason for excluding him from the UK when there is nothing in our law to prevent those of his fellows who are citizens of this country from practising Scientology here".

Sir John noted that "the attitude of the general public in Britain to foreigners – and to a good many other questions – demonstrates conflicting feelings of friendliness and hostility. On the one hand, there is the centuries-old insular tradition of contempt for Dagoes, Frogs, Wops and other lesser breeds without the law, who should be allowed to come here only for brief periods on sufferance, and then go home where they came from and trouble us no more. On the other hand, there is the equally old tradition of welcome and hospitality, founded on a desire to learn from others, to widen our horizons, to enrich our experience and especially to help those who suffer persecution in their own countries.

"The policy of successive Home Secretaries has been informed, with few exceptions, by the better tradition of friendliness and hospitality which has been the foundation in turn for our long-established policies of tolerance and asylum. The general principle on which the Home Office has in fact (even if not in theory) acted for a very long time is that foreigners should be free to come and go through our ports of entry as they please, unless there is clear evidence that they are likely to do us some specific harm, such as the commission of crimes, political activity endangering national security, the passing on of contagious diseases, putting our own people out of work, or indigence as the result of which we shall find ourselves forced to support them. In my view, such a policy has been right in the past and is right at the present time; as the world becomes smaller and the mobility of its peoples greater, it becomes more rather than less important that we should encourage rather than restrict the free flow of people and ideas.

"Against that background, it seems to me wrong in

principle for the Secretary of State for Home Affairs to use his wide powers of exclusion against those Scientologists who happen to be foreigners or Commonwealth citizens, when there is no law which prevents their colleagues holding UK citizenship from believing in their theories or carrying on their practices here. If the practices of Scientology are thought to constitute a danger to our society sufficiently grave to warrant prohibition or control under the law, then it is for Parliament to make such a law and for the Executive to apply it impartially to Britons and foreigners alike within the confines of this country. But so long as none of our laws are being infringed, the classification of *foreign* Scientologists as 'undesirable aliens' so that they are forbidden entry through our ports, while the accident of birth permits those Scientologists who happen to be citizens of the United Kingdom to process and be processed here with impunity, seems to me to constitute a use of this discretionary power which is quite contrary to the traditional policy followed by successive Home Secretaries over many years."[6]

Besides recommending that Scientologists of foreign or Commonwealth nationality should henceforth be admitted to Britain as visitors on precisely the same footing as other people, Sir John said that in his view Scientologists who wished to come and work in the UK ought to be granted or refused a work permit on the same criteria as everyone else, and the fact that they or their proposed employers are Scientologists should be regarded as quite irrelevant.

The Report did not, however, favour admitting Scientologists as students, who under Britain's immigration laws, form a privileged class and are normally allowed to stay four times as long as the ordinary visitor. Sir John gave as his reason for this stricture the fact that on the evidence before him he was not satisfied that Scientology schools as then organized were bona fide educational establishments.

A second major recommendation contained in the

192-page Report was the proposal that legislation be passed, aimed at controlling the practice of psychotherapy for fee or reward. Under terms of the Act, a professional council would be set up to pass on the practitioner's qualifications.

Was Sir John being naïve or merely clever when he advanced the absurd notion that such a professional council – probably controlled by psychiatrists and medical men – would, as he put it, welcome the Scientologists with open arms if they could make good their claim that Scientology was indeed the first thoroughly validated psychotherapy?

Did he honestly believe, after reviewing the documented evidence placed in his hands during the Inquiry, that the secret international alliance which had initiated the persecution of Scientologists all over the world would accept them as qualified colleagues?

Even allowing for the fact that the legal mind is capable of the most extraordinary contortions, one is driven to conclude that the eminent expert on law saw in such legislation the means of eliminating all unorthodox mental therapies.

Further supporting this view is the fact that he wanted the law to apply not only to Scientologists, but to doctors, dentists, ministers of religion, social workers and marriage guidance counsellors as well. "If any of these wish to charge their patients or clients for practicing psychotherapy on them, there is no reason why they should not first satisfy the Council that they have undergone the necessary training and obtained the necessary qualifications."

The residual import of Sir John's proposed legislation is that a protective trade union for psychotherapists, similar to that which exists for the practice of medicine, should be established by statute. There is abundant evidence to show that people whose minds and/or bodies have been seriously damaged by psychotherapy have been patients who were treated by the professional people Sir John would like to have determine the qualifications of others.

At the outset, Sir John states that since he held his

enquiry in private and heard neither witnesses nor advocates, he has considered himself disqualified from passing any judgment, adverse or favourable, on Scientology, its practitioners or practices. He nevertheless does pass judgment in the very thrust of his Report and in the selection of the material he presents. For example, he quotes a number of derogatory passages from the biased Anderson Report, referring to his Victorian colleague, as "Mr. Kevin Anderson, QC, a distinguished leader of the Melbourne Bar", presumably implying that the words of such an anointed member of his profession merit the kind of acceptance accorded a message from the Burning Bush.

He passes judgment on Scientology when he says, "I have been unable to discover any evidence which would support Scientology's claim to be a science . . ."[6] (p. 47)

He passed judgment on the leadership and practitioners of Scientology when he declared (in Paragraph 168, p. 120): "I am quite satisfied that the great majority of the *followers* [emphasis his] of Scientology are wholly sincere in their beliefs, show single-minded dedication to the subject, spend a great deal of money on it and are deeply convinced that it has proved of great benefit to them. But it is only fair also to make the obvious point that none of this furnishes evidence of the sincerity of the Scientology leadership, whose financial interests are the opposite of those of their followers."

Taken as a whole, the Foster Report clearly aims at denigrating Scientology, not in illuminating it.

Publicly, at least, the Scientologists themselves expressed great satisfaction with the Foster Report. David Gaiman, deputy guardian and Scientology's chief spokesman at the Saint Hill headquarters, told newsmen: "This has lifted a shadow that has been hanging over us for three years. Naturally, we are delighted that the report has recommended what we most wanted – that the ban on foreign Scientologists should be removed."

14—HSOS • •

From his flagship *Apollo*, L. Ron Hubbard issued a telex statement, saying: "I consider the lifting of the UK ban on Scientology's foreign students as a Christmas present.

"All the ban did was cost England many millions in foreign exchange and make unnecessary upsets for people. The ban never hurt Scientology. Its numbers are double those of 1968."

Hubbard said he felt no resentment towards the British Government, who had acted on reports now proven false. "I only hope this helps get German psychiatry off the backs of the British people."

The Scientologists' elation – if, indeed, it was genuine – was somewhat premature. A representative of the Home Office made it clear that the British Government had no intention of allowing foreign Scientologists back into Britain "in the foreseeable future".

Sir Keith Joseph, Secretary for Social Services, told the Commons that the main recommendation of the report was that the restrictions instituted in July 1968 should be relaxed, but that the practice of psychotherapy for reward should be restricted to suitably qualified persons. The Government took the view that the recommendations should be considered as a whole, that is, the ban could not be lifted until "after consultations with relevant professional organizations". "Until they are completed, the Goverment does not feel able to reach any conclusions on the report."

In a word, the ban which Sir John had found to be unjustified in the first place, *might be* lifted, but the Whitehall overlords had not decided in what century it might happen.

While the Scientologists regarded the Foster Report as a Christmas present to them, their indefatigable adversaries thought St. Nicholas had put *their* names on the package. In a letter dated December 29, 1971 to Mary Applebey, general secretary of the National Association for Mental

Health, Dr. D. H. Clark (medical superintendent of Fulbourn Hospital, Cambridge) wrote:

"I spent much of Christmas morning reading the Foster Report and as I read it in detail I was filled with un-Christmas glee. I may be wrong, but I believe that Sir John Foster has dealt Scientology a subtle but grievous wound from which they will suffer for many years.

"If one only reads the conclusions the report seems favourable to them. This is what David Gaiman (did you see him on TV?) and the Press and other superficial people immediately seized on and which caused the Scientologists to whoop with glee. Yet the conclusions could hardly have been otherwise. Callaghan's original decision to penalise the Scientologists – out of all the queer, religious and unpleasant political sects that come to Britain – could not, in the long term be defended. Apart from that, there was little for Sir John to make recommendations on, though his suggestion that the Tax Authorities screw down on all the shadow companies of the Scientologists will, I think, hurt them quite a bit in the long run.

"When one reads the whole report however, quite a different picture emerges; Sir John refuses to draw any specific conclusions; he expresses many doubts about the kind of enquiry that he has been holding, openly calling it 'Inquisitorial'; he says again and again that he will not publish any controversial evidence and he announces that he is going to destroy everything that was said to him yet to any dispassionate reader the endictment is wholly damning and this indictment is cunningly constructed of hardly anything but quotations from the Scientologists themselves. Sir John has cunningly extracted, from all the hundreds of documents that he must have had, examples of their vicious directives, evidence of their great wealth and cupidity and the very few really damaging incidents that are recorded against them (from the Anderson Report he lifts the one really terrifying story of how they processed a woman in front of Mr. Anderson to such an extent that she had to be admitted [to] a mental hospital a week later).

"I believe the total effect on any open-minded individual would be to damn the Scientologists utterly and I hope that as many people as possible – all Members of Parliament for instance – will read the report; I believe it is to them that Sir John was addressing himself. I believe that he concluded that the Scientology leadership were evil men, grasping, paranoid and litigious and that he decided to write a report for his own kind, Members of Parliament, Judges, Lawyers, members of the establishment which would slowly lead the reader to damn the Scientologists by quoting from their own texts. I may be imputing too much sublety to him but I cannot help wondering whether he did not deliberately refrain from condemning them in the hope that they would swallow the bait and endorse the report as they have done. I believe that he reached exactly the same conclusion as Mr. Anderson but decided that instead of launching a violent polemic against them which tends to be self-defeating (as the Anderson Report is in its very intemperance) he has written a seemingly temperate report which will do them much more harm in the long run.

"Certainly, they have swallowed the bait and have endorsed the report; we can now say to anyone who enquires 'Here is a Government Report on Scientology, the Scientologists have accepted it as fair, I suggest you read and come to your own conclusions!' "

Dr. Clark added: "If I am right in this I am sure that we ought to buy large numbers of copies of the Foster Report so that we will always have them available to lend to people when necessary. I think we should consider giving it the widest publicity possible. Could we perhaps consider devoting one copy of 'Mental Health' exclusively to quotations from the Foster Report – perhaps by using Sir John's techniques and adding nothing of our own but merely quoting from him?"

In her reply, Miss Appleby agreed that the Foster Report

was a subtle hatchet job, but she expressed some doubt that it had dealt as grievous a blow to the Scientologists as her comrade-in-arms seemed to think.

"I was delighted to have your Christmas lucubrations on the Foster Report, and I am delighted that you consider the Foster Report as subtle as I do. What I wonder is whether the wound you see is in fact very grievous. I entirely agree that there is nothing in the Report to cause the Scientologists glee. On the other hand, unless the public can be made to read the Report and to appreciate the subtlety of its conclusions, have we really got very far? Of course no objective enquirer could recommend that the immigration ban should be continued, but any suggestion that Dr. Weissmann and his merry men will deter the Scientologists from their 'therapy' is, I am afraid, moonshine (see Donald Gould in this week's *New Statesman*). However, it would be good to talk to you about this, as I am talking to a number of people."

The campaign to stamp out Scientology was still in full swing.

REFERENCE NOTES

1. *Freedom Scientology*, 1970.
2. *New York Times*, March 19, 1969.
3. Malcolm Muggeridge, *Tread Softly, For You Tread On My Jokes*. London: 1967.
4. *The Sun* (London) September 2, 1971.
5. *Sunday Tribune*, August 18, 1971.
6. *The Foster Report*. H.M. Printing Office, London: 1971.

10. *Privilege and Perjury in South Africa*

In South Africa, it was like watching a well-known play. The cast was different, but the lines were as familiar as those in the passage from *Macbeth*: "Tomorrow and tomorrow and tomorrow..." Anyone who had attended the performances in Melbourne, Adelaide, Perth and London could have joined in under his breath.

There on stage was the protagonist, the cosmic pretzelbender from the National Association for Mental Health (played by T. J. Stander) with his overblown rhetoric describing the horrors of Scientology.

There were the Pals in Parliament (Drs. Ventner and Vosloo, and the Hon. Mr. Wood) who duly raise the motions; the Honest Health Minister (Dr. Hertzog) who refuses to act on rumour and second-hand evidence of what allegedly happened in another country half a world away, and is forthwith supplanted by the Second Health Minister, (Dr. de Wet) an obedient servant.

Then, in their turn, come the Chief Headshrinker (Dr. Pascoe) who appears briefly to dispense learned nonsense

and dire warnings; the White Knights of Journalism following, ludicrously mounted on jackasses and bearing banners with such inscriptions as "Punish These People",
"Ban Scientology" and "Witchcraft Too"; and bringing up
the rear, the long-faced clergy (the Reverends de Vos,
Botha and van Niekerk) reciting the Word of God, spiced
with such pulpit metaphors as "Synagogue of Satan".

Providing an absurdist background of camouflage and
confusion to the whole performance is the Anvil Chorus
(Rational Thinkers, National Welfare Board members,
Professors of psychology, and Medical Association lobbyists) all in fright wigs, intoning passages from the
Anderson Report, like a group of Maoists brandishing the
little red book.

The entire production is centred, of course, upon the
Inquiry, which comes along in due course, and apparently
is intended to supply an element of suspense. The False
Witness (Capt. Jan Hendrick du Plessis) gives perjured
evidence which two and a half years later he will recant, as
did Phil Wearne in Australia, saying he was motivated by a
desire for revenge. Testimony will be taken from outraged
parents and marriage partners, failed Scientologists, an
ex-Communist, alcoholics and psychiatric patients.

Although there were a few random laughs imparted by
befuddled stand-up comics in baggy trousers; and fragile
hysterics when Possessive Mother with voice vibrating like
violin strings, told how Scientology lured her forty-five-
year-old son away from home, on the whole the South
African performance was a mechanical replay, put on by an
amateur dramatic society.

Viewing it, one sometimes longed for the vigorous, even
if vulgar, delivery of a Gordon Just; or the Freudian
thousand-and-one nights of a Douglas Moon down under.

T. J. Stander, who has played the leading role in the
South African extravaganza, began preparing for the
pageant as far back as 1960. On November 22 of that year,

he wrote a letter to the Group for the Advancement of Psychiatry in New York, asking that organization what steps they had taken against Scientology, explaining that "in terms of existing legislation in South Africa, no steps can be taken to debar Scientologists from practicing, although we are worried in the extreme about the activities of this body". Stander's signature identified him as organizing secretary of the S.A. National Council for Mental Health.

Identical letters were sent to the Philippine Mental Health Association; the National Association for Mental Health (UK); the Department of National Health and Welfare (Canada), and to the American Medical Association.

With the dedicated zeal of a latter-day Savanarola, Stander also began to organize the potential opposition to Scientology at home. On December 7, 1961, he sent a memorandum to all members of the Executive Committee (South African National Council for Mental Health) and to all mental health societies in the Republic, asking them to submit to him information appearing in local papers and magazines, concerning "courses in psychology and related subjects".

Typical of the material being garnered by Stander was an exchange of correspondence between Dr. Scott Millar, medical officer of health for the city of Johannesburg and the Hubbard Association of Scientologists. Millar had written the Scientologists, soliciting information concerning Scientology. After receiving it, he wrote the Scientology organization that "I have read some of these pamphlets and consider that as an example of meretricious pseudo-science Scientology would be hard to beat and that the claims made for it are not only ridiculous [sic] but an insult to the intelligence of any normal person."

Dr. Millar closed his letter with a threat: "I propose to report your activities to the authorities concerned for any action they may wish to take on the matter."

In keeping with Scientology's policy of giving as good as, if not better, than they received, Mary Sue Hubbard replied: "As you have no knowledge as to what Scientology is or what Scientology does, then such a report as you mention you intend to make to the concerned authorities would be more meretricious nonsense and more irresponsibly damaging perhaps to your own position as Medical Officer of Health than your opinion of Scientology is to Scientology and those of us who work in it."

Her letter concluded: "Please understand that our concern in this matter is merely that you, knowing nothing of Scientology, have no right to condemn it or not condemn it, and particularly as you hold a public position of responsibility, you, in particular should be much more careful of what statement you make."

When it came to employing the technique of the noiseless, patient spider, T. J. Stander had no equal among anti-Scientology plotters. He tirelessly wrote memoranda and letters. He sponsored and helped co-ordinate informal evening talks on Scientology. He acted as liaison among various medical, psychological and social welfare groups. He solicited and had printed or reprinted articles hostile to Scientology. He planted a spy in the Scientology organization with orders to entrap the adherents. He spent hours on the telephone to members of various "scientific bodies", urging them to "use your knowledge and influence of your position to take action against this organization". In July 1961, he told Dr. A. B. Daneel of Sterkfontein Hospital — another volunteer Scientology fighter:

"I have had the affairs of these people investigated. A detailed memorandum is being prepared for submission to the Ministers of Justice, Health and Education, Arts and Science. A deputation representing my council, the Medical Association of South Africa, the Psychological Association of South Africa, and the S.A. National Council for Child Welfare, will meet the Ministers concerned to press for legislation declaring not only Scientologists International, but also the Psychology Foundation of South Africa, illegal."

In early April 1966, South African newspapers carried a story stating that leading psychologists "and other mental specialists" in Johannesburg, Durban and Cape Town were investigating the activities of the Scientologists and that the Psychological Association of South Africa would shortly issue its findings. It was suggested that the report would be "quite startling".

However, the Scientologists promptly announced that investigation was a game any number could play, and that they had set up a team of investigators to probe the activities of certain psychiatrists practicing in Durban, Johannesburg and other South African centres. Dossiers on some of the practitioners had already been compiled and were in the hands of L. Ron Hubbard.

So far as I am able to determine, the shocking exposé promised by the Psychological Association never materialized.

Following the original scenario, Dr. E. L. Fisher, Member for Rosettenville, on September 30, 1966, arose in Parliament to ask Dr. Albert Hertzog, the Minister of Health, the customary question: had his attention been drawn to a cult being practised in the Republic under the name of Hubbard Association of Scientologists International, and whether his department had investigated the cult in relation to the people's health. If he had not done so, would he now have such an investigation made?

The answer was that the Health Ministry had made a preliminary investigation of Scientology, but that it had turned up no tangible facts requiring any official action.

Undaunted, Dr. Fisher was on his feet again in the House of Assembly two weeks later, asking whether the Health Minister had received further communications in regard to Scientology, and pressing for an inquiry.

Dr. Hertzog replied that he had received only two letters

from individuals, one in praise of Scientology and one against it. Until more convincing evidence could be put forward, there was no justification for a full-scale inquiry.

So the wind blew and the worlds flew, and there again stood the Hon. Member for Rosettenville, on May 4, 1967, putting down Scientology. The cult, said he, could use information obtained during the "security check", made at the beginning of the course, to blackmail anyone answering the questions for the rest of his life. He also quoted the standard passages from the Anderson Report and then, on cue, called once more for an official inquiry into Scientology.

Dr. Hertzog said in reply that one could not rely solely upon the Anderson Report as a basis for launching a Government inquiry in South Africa. He needed information from people who had allegedly been victimized by Scientology. He simply did not have a prima facie case needed to justify an inquiry.

Dr. Hertzog later told a newsman: "We must be very careful not to have inquisitions against people. This is not a police state. Overseas government commission findings are not sufficient proof."

Such, however, was not the thinking of the National Association for Mental Health and of that organization's Pals in Parliament. Two weeks later, Dr. Fisher once again, during a debate on another Health Department issue, urged the Health Minister "to find some way of assisting persons suffering from the persecutions of Scientologists".

And once more Dr. Hertzog answered that if anyone would provide him with evidence that Scientology was harmful, an investigation would be justified; but no such evidence had been forthcoming.

As a matter of fact, Dr. Hertzog went on, when it became known that Dr. Fisher would introduce a motion against Scientology during the previous parliamentary session, the Health Minister had been astonished by the number of persons in high positions who had approached him to tell him of the benefits they were deriving from Scientology.

It must have occurred to T.J. Stander and associates that their failure to get official action in Parliament was attributable to the fact that they were represented by the Opposition.

Stander told a visiting French psycho-therapist that "the Government will never decide to accept a motion presented by anyone of the Opposition".

The only way to accomplish their purpose, Stander continued, would be to enlist the help of a Member who was a Nationalist. The man they had in mind was Dr. W. L. D. M. Venter, for Kimberley South.

"I would appreciate it," Stander told his visitor who, during their conversation, had demonstrated an expert knowledge of the subject, "if you could instruct Dr. Venter on Scientology because he knows nothing about it, or very little – and myself also; the only thing I know about it is what I learned in England during my travels overseas, and it's very little. Then we're going to arrange a meeting with Mr. Venter and this time it is going to be a serious business. We have two months for that, and not a minute to lose."

While preparations went forward on this new front, the South African press launched a massive assault on Scientology, making use of the traditional weapons – rumour bombardment and the poison gas of "expert opinion". Scientologists were depicted as "a back-slapping crowd", intolerant, self-righteous, vindictive, who "seemed able to disregard many traditional moral concepts and the normal community's sense of values". They broke up marriages and alienated families. They caused mental breakdowns: "The condition of a man who had suffered from schizophrenia was much aggravated. He is now completely dependent on psychiatric treatment – a Jekyll and Hyde personality."

A seventeen-year-old Durban youth, whom the *Sunday*

Tribune described as a "schoolboy" who had taken an introductory course in Scientology, was quoted as saying that two women Scientologists "grilled" him about intimate details of his sex life.

"One of the women, he said, asked him if he enjoyed sex and then demanded: 'Do you want to go to bed with me?' At another time she hurled four-letter words at him – while a six-year old child stood by, listening."

The *Eastern Province Herald* of Port Elizabeth, reprinted portions of a scurrilous article that had appeared in the *Women's Wear Daily* in New York, labelling Scientology a high-priced confidence game, and asserting that "it worships no god but its founder, L. Ron Hubbard, a sort of Western guru with an unholy smile". Scientologists were described as "flower children, hippies, high school dropouts and disillusioned adults. One of the principal 'dynamics' or commandments for the cult's worshippers is the sex act itself, pure and simple."

On a popular level, in South Africa, where last year alone, a reported 200,000 white weekend swingers ducked over the border into black Swaziland to partake of forbidden fruit (striptease, pornographic books, casino gambling, and racially mixed fun and games), such pungent copy was more likely to arouse interest than to excite indignation. But the group seeking to crush Scientology correctly reasoned that such lurid charges would soften up Members of Parliament who, in their role of law-givers, had to put on the robes of righteousness.

To lend an air of intellectual respectability to what was in fact an unmitigated campaign of mud-slinging, Stander and his associates provided a roster of psychiatrists, leading political figures and university professors to appear before students' associations and public discussion groups, where they gave "objective" analyses of Scientology.

An organization known as the Rational Thinkers Forum announced that it would conduct a full inquiry into Scientology, but drew in its horns when Scientologists made

it clear they would hold the "investigators" legally responsible for their statements.

The Cape Town *Evening Post* published a story based on
a statement by the Forum Chairman, Mrs. Lily Paltiel,
saying that prominent people would be asked to give
evidence before an investigating committee which would sit
in camera. The investigators would include "doctors, philosophers, a minister of religion and a sociologist". Members
of the public who wished to give evidence were directed
to write to the Investigating Committee, Rational Thinkers
Forum, P.O. Box 10086, Cape Town.

Later, when interviewed by a Scientology staff member
concerning the project, Mrs. Paltiel denied that the
Rational Thinkers were planning anything like an investigation of Scientology. What they had in mind was merely
"a symposium of objective opinions aimed at imparting
accurate facts".

On April 8, 1968, the *Evening Post* ran a retraction of its
earlier story, saying that the Forum would not conduct an
inquiry as reported by the paper in its weekend edition of
March 9. Instead, it would hold a symposium on the
subject of Scientology.

In what was clearly a move to make certain that they did
not have to confront Scientology's lawyers in court, the
Rational Thinkers changed even the title of their
"Symposium Scientology" to the more generalized one of
"Brainwashing".

In a circular letter to members, Mrs. Paltiel rationally
explained: "We just dare not ask you to spend an entire
evening listening to the promises Scientologists do (or do
not) keep. One actually needs to adhere to that cult to
acquire so much endurance. And why should we restrict
ourselves to a mere aspect of a wide subject?"

The representatives of enlightened opinion who provided
the answers at the symposium were Dr. F. D. Pascoe,
senior psychiatrist in Government Service; Dr. F. J. M.
Potgieter, psychologist and professor of theology at the

University of Stellenbosch; and Mrs. Catherine Taylor, MP for Wynberg.

The illustrious speakers equated Scientology processing with brainwashing, and attacked the E-meter as a misleading diagnostic tool.

In her address, the Hon. Mrs. Taylor imputed to Scientology the evils most characteristic of psychoanalysis rather than of Scientology. "When the anxiety of any client is made use of by means of lengthy and costly consultations and a physical diagnosis is only reached after a long period of time – this is a confidence trick in the accepted sense of the word."

Dr. Pascoe, Senior Psychiatrist in Government Service, spoke of the methods used by a brainwasher whose intention was evil, and gave the rough side of his tongue to "those leaders of cults who start their own cult in the hope of acquiring wealth and power over the lives of others". The scientific quality of Dr. Pascoe's discourse (and perhaps of the entire evening) can best be savoured in his concluding remarks:

"Brainwashing is a good thing in good hands, an evil thing in evil hands. This laundress, this dainty little lady who washes brains, she wears many clothes; she comes like Eve with many apples in her hand. Don't let her deceive you."

The final push towards Governmental action against Scientology came in the early part of 1969. A number of leading South African newspapers ran lengthy statements "to urge, in the highest circles, an enquiry into Scientology".

In a front-page leader, *Die Transvaler* said the demand for an official inquiry had the support of church leaders, and introduced a racial note into the issue. Scientology, it said, "has an ethical precept which is in conflict with the Christian Ethic, and propagates an inherent liberalistic attitude of equality of rights for all races and colours".

Early in February 1969, T. J. Stander met with Dr. Venter in Pretoria and gave him a file of documents and press cuttings concerning Scientology. Among the papers turned over to the MP was the draft of a motion to be made in Parliament asking for an official inquiry into Scientology.

A week later, Dr. Venter presented a private motion in the House of Assembly calling for an investigation into the activities of Scientology with a view to banning the organization in South Africa.

In the three-hour debate which followed, Scientology's familiar enemies, protected by Parliamentary privilege, spoke with militant mouths. "We must decide," said Dr. W. L. Vosloo, Nationalist MP for Brentwood, "if this monstrosity – this octopus – is a religion as it claims to be."

Mrs. C. D. Taylor declared that Scientology was "silly and sick" and represented a danger to psychologically unstable people.

Nor was that all. Particularly disturbing, said Mr. L. F. Wood (U.P., Berea) had been reports from overseas about the organization's approach to sex. South Africa could not dismiss the situation lightly. As for the founder of the cult, Ron Hubbard, there was ample evidence that he was an impostor and a fraud.

After the Honourable Members had roundly condemned the practices, founder, aims and potentialities of Scientology – both in South Africa and abroad – it was Dr. Carel de Wet's turn. Dr. de Wet was the newly appointed Minister of Health who, unlike his predecessor, was willing to appoint a Commission of Inquiry into Scientology because objections against the organization "have been raised in responsible quarters". Referring to the action taken against Scientology by the Government of Great Britain, Dr. de Wet offered his clencher: "If Britain acts, then you must know that the hour is late."

A month later, on March 28, 1969, the South African Government appointed a nine-member Commission of

Inquiry into Scientology, under the chairmanship of G. P. C. Kotze, a former Supreme Court Judge.

The other members of the Commission were, by profession and social background persons likely to be hostile to Scientology. There were: the Rev. G. J. Davidtz, minister of the Nederduitse Kerk, and Welfare Board executive; Professor A. J. van Wyk, Deputy Commissioner of Mental Health and senior psychiatrist at Weskoppies Hospital; Prof. I. J. J. van Rooyen, head of the department of Social Work, Rand Afrikaanse University; Dr. L. van Z. Pretorius, who formerly lectured at Stellenbosch University; Prof. G. A. Elliott, member of the Medicine Control Board, for twenty-one years associated with the medical faculty of Witwatersrand University; Prof. H. L. Swanepoel, dean of the law faculty at the University of Potchefstroom; P. E. Bosman, ex-secretary of Social Welfare and Pensions; and Mrs. A. M. G. Maytom, career politician and former mayoress of Durban.

Leading the evidence before the Commission, E. O. K. Harwood, Attorney-General for the Eastern Cape, fell easily into the role of prosecutor. Like Gordon Just, who had played the part in the original Melbourne production, the style and idiom of Harwood's utterances marked him as a Grand Inquisitor.

He challenged the testimony of pro-Scientology witnesses and treated that of their adversaries with gentle deference. On one occasion he suggested to a Scientologist who was giving evidence that the movement may have relegated Hubbard to the position of founder or "father figure" because he had become an embarrassment to them.

Scientologists had no illusions about what they should expect from those who sat in the seats of the mighty; but with one eye on that greater tribunal, the public, they presented their best advocates, flown in from various parts of the world to give evidence.

Producers of the South African show no doubt welcomed the appearance of the distinguished witnesses from overseas because they lent an international flavour and importance to proceedings which in themselves were of very limited interest.

Among the foreign witnesses who spoke on Scientology's behalf were Dr. Thomas S. Szasz, noted psychiatrist upon whose unique work I have drawn heavily in the preceding pages; John J. Matonis, chairman of the American Trial Lawyers Association; Prof. Harold Kaufman, a lawyer-psychiatrist of Washington, D.C.; Dr. Edward Hamlyn, a British physician, specializing in psychosomatic illnesses; and David B. Gaiman, Deputy Guardian of the Church of Scientology (World Wide), East Grinstead.

The evidence given by these expert witnesses from abroad was unequivocal and outspoken. For that reason, it stirred interest and was fully reported in the press.

Dr. Szasz told the Commission that, while he was not himself a Scientologist, he agreed to a large extent with the movement's attack on psychiatry. He said the practice of involuntary psychiatry was a communistic ideology and that psychiatry was making "a cancerous invasion" of the law, politics and religion in America. Striking close to home, Dr. Szasz informed the commissioners that in some quarters in the U.S., racism was assumed to be symptomatic of mental disease.

Mr. Matonis upset the commissioners' comfortable conclusion that Scientology was not a religion by citing the case of Aaron Barr, a young ministerial student whom a New York Court of Appeal had granted exemption from military service on the ground that he was a duly ordained Scientology minister.

Dr. Hamlyn likewise dealt harshly with the well-settled notion that there was something about Scientology that was disastrously harmful to health. Only a few days previously Dr. M. G. Feldman, spokesman for the Medical Association of South Africa, had testified that Scientology, "with its confused application of confused concepts", could be harmful.

Dr. Hamlyn said Scientology had provided him the answer to treating psychosomatic illness, which he had been seeking for twenty years. After taking a course in Dianetics, he had decided that the system would be of enormous value to the medical profession and took another course which qualified him to train others in Dianetic auditing.

David Gaiman, a man of subtle intelligence, who heads Scientology's public relations worldwide, countered the thrusts of Dr. Harwood, counsel for the Commission, with ripostes worthy of the most accomplished verbal fencing master.

Referring to the Scientology policy letter cancelling rules relating to second dynamic activities, the counsel asked Mr. Gaiman if that did not "put a premium on fornication".

Gaiman replied in the famous words of Edward III, now the motto of Britain's Order of the Garter: *Honi soit qui mal y pense* (Evil to him who evil thinks).

In another exchange, Harwood asked the Scientology spokesman what reason T. J. Stander (director of the South African Council for Mental Health) could have for maliciously attacking Scientology as the witness had testified. Gaiman replied that "no reason is unreason", and suggested that he could not go beyond this without tarnishing somebody's reputation.

As David Gaiman had no doubt foreseen, Harwood pressed him to give his opinion, assuring him that anything defamatory would be privileged testimony in the setting of an official inquiry.

Gaiman then stated: "Unless Mr. Stander is a Communist, I find it difficult to see why malice should bite so deep."

Thus far, two of the principal witnesses against Scientology have given sworn statements retracting their testimony before the Commission.

One of them, a private secretary named Eileen Drummond, stated in her affidavit that her assertions at the

Inquiry to the effect that Scientology was responsible for family upsets and had changed her daughter for the worse, were false.

Mrs. Drummond declared that her statement that her daughter had cut herself off from her because of Scientology's policy of disconnection should be clarified. "I am clear in my own mind that the reason she seldom contacted me had nothing to do with the philosophy or policy of Scientology."

Even more startling was the recantation of Jan Hendrik du Plessis, former police captain, who had been the featured witness against Scientology.

During his appearance before the Commission, du Plessis had aired a series of unsubstantiated charges and personal opinions aimed at creating suspicion and dread of Scientology. At one point, he even submitted a book on the life and practices of Aleister Crowley, the notorious British Satanist (known as "the wickedest man in the world") and asserted that Hubbard had once been his disciple. Although there was no reference of any kind in the book, either to Hubbard or to Scientology, Commission Chairman Kotze accepted the volume in evidence.

Apparently in a penitential mood two and a half years later, du Plessis retracted the evidence he had given. In an astonishing affidavit sworn to on February 3, 1972, he stated that his testimony before the Commission had been biased, misleading, untrue, and motivated by a desire for revenge. Among the specific false allegations cited in his lengthy recantation were the following:

"I believe the statements I made with regard to the religious nature of Scientology to be misleading. The facts I reported about the Church selling its property as being a purely business proposition and this being an indication that this was contrary to the behaviour of a religious body had nothing whatsoever to do with the issue at hand and were made solely with the intent to slander the Church.

"The statements I made in testimony comparing the

organisations of Scientology with the criminal organisation commonly known as the Mafia were completely unwarranted and completely false in material facts, namely:

(*a*) Scientology organisations have never to my knowledge used blackmail, and I have never found or been presented with any evidence at any time suggesting otherwise.

(*b*) I do not in fact know of any case where it was required that a Scientologist had to renounce his earlier religion.

(*c*) My statement that Scientologists at Saint Hill Manor engaged in sex orgies is completely without foundation in fact.

"The story which I related before the Commission that I had been followed, and subjected to anonymous and threatening telephone calls is false in all details and was stated by myself to lend credence to my earlier statements about the use of intimidation by the Scientology organisation, of which I have no evidence of any kind whatsoever.

"I gave considerable testimony relating to an article published in the *Sunday Times* (a London newspaper) which claimed to connect L. Ron Hubbard with the black magician, Aleister Crowley, namely.

(*a*) I claimed to have sighted letters in L. Ron Hubbard's handwriting, addressed to Crowley. This is false, there being no such letters.

(*b*) I said that Crowley was L. Ron Hubbard's master, when as pointed out by the *Sunday Times* retraction article, this is completely untrue.

(*c*) I stated that there was no court case over the *Sunday Times* article. This is incorrect. Legal action was started but was settled out of court with the *Sunday Times* publishing a full correction of the original article.

"I stated in the course of the Commission hearing that

some of L. Ron Hubbard's writings were 'the ravings of a diseased mind'. This is not true and I apologise for the statement unreservedly.

"I said that on visiting the London premises of the Church of Scientology one evening, I found it full of people sleeping on the floor and on benches, which is an untrue statement. I also stated that a London police official told me that they knew about this and that the police raided the organisation every so often. This is definitely not true and in fact the London Scientology organisation has never been raided to my knowledge."

As I write, three years have elapsed since the Inquiry was initiated, but the Commission has not issued a report. The South African speech and drama festival continues. When the final curtain descends on that stage, it will no doubt rise elsewhere for yet another run.

Advance men are already at work in Holland, for example, where as yet there are not more than a hundred Scientologists in the entire country. When a small Scientology mission was established in the Netherlands in 1970, the British National Association for Mental Health arranged a meeting between their representatives and officers of their Dutch counterpart. One of the latter, was the publisher of the newspaper *Vrij Nederland*, which soon thereafter launched an attack on Scientology, based in part upon material obtained by intimidation from Dutch Scientologists.

There are indications that in the future, the assault on Scientology will be handled in a less obvious and more indirect way. In the Province of Ontario, Canada and in Rhodesia, a law to restrict the practice of psychology has been drafted. In both countries the measures, based partly on the Victorian legislation, ostensibly regulate the practice of psychology, but are sufficiently broad in terms of reference to include Scientology.

In fact, during the Parliamentary debate in Rhodesia, one

of the Senators complained that "the present definition of psychological practices as appearing in the Bill, which is a verbatim representation of the definition which appeared in the Victoria Act, is a definition of so wide a scope that it would be almost impossible to imagine any communication between one human being and another not to be psychological practice".

A study commissioned by the Province of Ontario and carried out by Prof. John A. Lee of Toronto, included not only Scientologists, but also sectarian healers (such as Christian Scientists and Spiritualists) whom medical and psychiatric practitioners would like to see suppressed.

It remains to ask: can the embattled Scientologists survive in their heroic resistance against the organized might of their powerful enemies throughout the world?

L. Ron Hubbard believes they can. "Our opponents," he said, "are a small clique running against the trend of the world. They will lose."

I am inclined to agree. As London columnist C. H. Rolph once aptly observed: Scientology is an anvil that will wear out all the hammers.

Epilogue

Since being written, events have rolled on.

The FDA case has resulted in a major win for the Scientologists. All the materials looted from the Founding Church in January 1963, have had to be returned by the FDA to the Church.

In Australia, Federal recognition of the Church has led to the repeal of the West Australian Act against Scientology.

Another major win by the Church—and credit to the Government in Western Australia.

In South Australia, Repeal is on the Parliamentary Order Paper and is expected to go through Parliament shortly: again, a nice win for the Scientologists.

Western Australia has also dropped the proscription on the word "Scientology"—another Scientology win.

In Victoria, relations between the Church and the Government have broken through the prior ice pack, and are the best for 10 years.

Predictably, South Africa published the report on the inquiry, omitting totally, evidence from Dr. T. Szasz or the documented evidence on Mr. T. J. Stander. No action on the report has been taken by the new Minister of Health— no doubt due to the retractions by two principal anti-Scientology witnesses: a welcome boost for Scientologists in South Africa.

In England, two books concerning the Scientology fight on Rights for the mentally ill have both commented very favourably on the steps and actions taken by the Church. The National Association for Mental Health now prefers to be known as 'MIND', and Miss Mary Applebey, one of the key antagonists against the Scientologists, quietly left the National Association in December 1973.

On February 14, 1974, the British Home Office opposed the Scientologists in their plea to take the alien ban restrictions to the European Court of Justice in Luxembourg. The Home Office had argued that its view was so clearly right as to preclude the necessity of the case going to Luxembourg. "I am wholly unable to accept that contention", said Mr. Justice Pennycuick, who allowed the Scientologists to make a historical precedent by being the first British organization ever to refer a case to Luxembourg.

The case will be heard in six months' time or so. Meanwhile it is yet another victory for the Scientologists.

And finally, the biennial reference guide, the Encyclopedia Britannica Year Book, stated that Scientology was the 'largest of the new religions'.

REFERENCE NOTES FOR CHAPTER 6

1. Hannah Arendt, *The Origins of Totalitarianism.* N.Y.: 1951.
2. *The Findings on the U.S. Food and Drug Industry.* Scientology publication.
3. Rev. Robert H. Thomas, "Religion, Liberty and the FDA", in *Attack On A Church*, a Scientology publication.
4. *Sherbert v. Verner*, 374 U.S. at 407.
5. *West Virginia State Board of Education v. Barnette*, 319 U.S. 624, 642, 63 S. Ct. 1178, 87L.Ed. 1628 (1943).
6. 409 F2d. 1161.
7. *Washington Post*, July 1, 1967.